THE PROCUREMENT OF LIBRARY FURNISHINGS
Specifications, Bid Documents, and Evaluation

The Procurement
of Library Furnishings

Specifications,
Bid Documents,
and Evaluation

Proceedings of the

Library Equipment Institute

conducted at New York, N.Y.

July 7-9, 1966

Sponsored by the

Library Administration
Division

American Library Association

Edited by Frazer G. Poole and

Alphonse F. Trezza

AMERICAN LIBRARY ASSOCIATION

Chicago 1969

Standard Book Number 8389-3093-X (1969)
Library of Congress Catalog Card Number 70-77274
Copyright © 1969 by the American Library Association
Manufactured in the United States of America

Preface

More than five hundred librarians, trustees, architects, consultants, and representatives of manufacturers supplying equipment to the profession attended the third Institute on Library Equipment sponsored by the Equipment Committee of the Library Administration Division, American Library Association, which was held July 7-9, 1966, at the Statler-Hilton Hotel, New York, New York. The areas covered in this Institute are those of preparing contracts and purchase orders, writing bid documents, problems in the preparation of specifications, and testing and value analysis. The papers herein present the views of the speakers, and are not necessarily those of the American Library Association.

The first Institute on Library Equipment was held in Coral Gables (June 14-16, 1962) and dealt with furniture and bookstack selection, equipment and methods in catalog card reproduction, and photocopying from bound volumes and microtext. The second Institute, held in St. Louis (June 26-27, 1964), was concerned with matters of illumination, flooring, informal furnishings, and listening facilities. These three Institute proceedings constitute a series of important papers and discussions covering major areas of library equipment.

The thanks and appreciation of the Equipment Committee are due Mr. Bernard Wysocki, Director of Purchases, Brooklyn Public Library, as Chairman of the Equipment Institute and Mr. Frazer G. Poole, then Librarian of the University of Illinois Library, Chicago Circle Campus, as Chairman of the Equipment Committee who carefully planned the program and selected the speakers.

Appreciation is also due the members of the Division staff for the excellent hotel arrangements and for the efficient handling of matters relating to advance planning, registration, and finances.

ALPHONSE F. TREZZA
Associate Executive Director
for Administrative Services
formerly Executive Secretary
August 28, 1968   Library Administration Division

AMERICAN LIBRARY ASSOCIATION

Library Administration Division

Section on Buildings and Equipment

Roger B. Francis, Chairman
Director
South Bend Public Library
South Bend, Indiana

Donald C. Davidson, Vice-Chairman
Librarian
University of California Library
Santa Barbara, California

Helen A. Young, Secretary
Director
Hennepin County Library
Minneapolis, Minnesota

Committees

Architecture Committee for Public Libraries
Jasper Wright, Chairman
Assistant Director
South Bend Public Library
South Bend, Indiana

Building Committee for College and University Libraries
Clyde L. Haselden, Chairman
Librarian
Lafayette College Library
Easton, Pennsylvania

Building Committee for Hospital, Institution, and Special Libraries
Roderick Swartz, Chairman
Assistant Director
Tulsa City-County Library System
Tulsa, Oklahoma

Equipment Committee
Frazer G. Poole, Chairman
Director, Library
University of Illinois, Chicago Circle
Chicago, Illinois

Planning School Library Quarters Committee
Dr. Miriam E. Peterson, Chairman
Director
Division of Libraries
Chicago Board of Education
Chicago, Illinois

Equipment Institute Chairman
Bernard Wysocki
Director of Purchases
Brooklyn Public Library
Brooklyn, New York

Alphonse F. Trezza, Executive Secretary
Robert J. Shaw, Assistant to the Executive Secretary

Contents

Library Furnishings and Equipment

FRANCIS R. ST. JOHN
Library Consultants, Inc.
Brooklyn, New York

There are some things which this Library Equipment and Building Institute has done over the years, and some things which it has not done. It has been instrumental in bringing together thinking librarians, thinking designers, thinking architects, and people who are about to spend money on buildings. As a result of bringing these people together, a new concept of library equipment has begun to emerge. On the basis of the reports written on each Institute, one would think this concept has become nationwide. It has not, and I will go into that later.

This library institute has precipitated much of the progressive thinking that has gone into furniture and equipment design. However, furniture and equipment design still is not too far from the traditional. We are still thinking in terms of the library we have had for the last twenty-five or fifty years. That library is changing very rapidly, however. I wonder if you realize that your designs may not be changing fast enough to catch up?

The Library Technology Project, the testing laboratories which have been employed, and the materials from this meeting are going to give a great deal of detail on what is being done to ensure a good product. There are still many flaws in buying methods, and I am not sure you are going to be able to do much about them. For example, if the purchases are made by a purchasing agent for a city or college or other institution, with little or no concern for the library, the librarian, architect, and designer are not going to have much to say about what is bought. Buying is not always a matter of getting the lowest bid. It is not a matter of saying this specification "or equal," because I have seen too many of these specifications that are meaningless. Quite often the interpretation of what you want is not carried by the specifications.

Perhaps having the equipment institute one year and the building institute the next means that the information they present does not reach as many people as it should. My guess is that the Proceedings of these institutes do not get distribution beyond the people who attend because they are too expensive. Library trustees and other people who should be getting them in the outskirts, in the places where libraries are needed, do not have access to them unless they borrow them. If you have a really up-and-coming library and have a library consultant working with you, he will bring in some of this material.

There are about 450 persons, I have been told, registered at this preconference institute. I do not know how many libraries there are represented. I have met some of my friends from Canada here, so I know that more than the United States is represented. All kinds of libraries from two countries are represented.

I have been around these countries in the last two years as a library consultant. I have seen things that most of you are not willing to admit. I have seen a library planned for a college that was just starting given space that was already too small when the college began. The librarian was told that, in time, the library could expand to upper floors in the building and then to the entire building, if necessary. The engineer in the college, not the architect, decided to put the boiler and power equipment on the second floor, and the place for this library to expand was to the third floor. But there was no access from the first to the third floor.

In this same library the librarian had insisted on dull-surface tables so that there would be no glare. I walked in through the front door of that library and the glare was so bad I had to put on dark glasses before I got into the reading room. Neither the librarian nor the architect was given any opportunity to decide what kind of equipment was going to be used. The reading tables had the highest gloss finish I have ever seen, with high-intensity light above them. You can imagine trying to read on that kind of a table. Yet every table in this college reading room was the same. I am not exaggerating.

I have been in other libraries where makeshift had to do. The planners had not made the best use of the tax money that was available. They could have, if they had utilized proper library equipment. There are a lot of representatives of firms here, but they do not cover the country as I do. I have seen a library in a school situated on the stage of the auditorium. There were only folding chairs in it because every time the auditorium was used, the chairs had to be moved aside and a curtain pulled across the books. The people in charge thought they were doing well because they had a library, and they did have better than nothing.

When one talks here about equipment and about the kind of testing done, and one sees poor equipment around this country and Canada, it is evident that some people with funds available have not always purchased the most advantageous equipment. Sometimes the best and lowest bids may look good, but they do not always stand up. I heard about one bid for furniture that went to the lowest bidder. The furniture was good-looking, it fit in with the design of the new building, but in less than a year, the chairs were falling apart.

What is your protection against a situation like that? Can you protect your library against it through this organization? I wish you could. There *are* ways of doing it, but meeting once a year to talk about what would be nice to have is not the answer. I think that you are going to have to get up in arms to find out what can be done.

I suspect that this audience is made up of three different kinds of people: one, the people who are here because they come every year; two, those who have goods that they would like to get into the library market; and three, the people who either are thinking of building or have money enough to build, with a sprinkling of a few others.

I think it is a shame that a professional organization still has the task to create an image of the library as a warm kind of place. There are many beautiful libraries that attract people by the looks of the building, the equipment, the arrangement, the audio-visual facilities, the layout, the site, the color, the combination of all these things. But my experience has been

that there are many places where this image has not been created and where the effects of these Institutes have not reached. I am hoping that what may come out of these discussions in the next few days is not that each of you will absorb for yourself a few more points, a few more ideas about how to test, a few more ideas on why some wood finishes are better than others, but that you will develop a pioneer or a missionary spirit so that you can carry back into your own communities a zeal to make sure that the results of this meeting are put into practice.

Now, let me give you a suggestion on how this can be done. I have a copy of the report of the last equipment institute. It took a long while to produce and cost a lot of money. Most of the smaller libraries were not able to buy it. It seems to me that there should be some way in which this Library Equipment Institute, with so many people coming and examining equipment, should be able to provide money for distribution of the Proceedings. If not, then petition ALA to produce a little brochure that can be circulated on a wider basis. The brochure could give people an idea of what library equipment, library color, and library arrangement should be in order to be effective and to do the job that a modern library should perform. Making this information available is a serious matter to me.

I am saying this because I have seen so much, so very much, of the opposite. I have seen a public library in a broom closet on the second floor of a school. And I dare any of you to match anything like that.

Contracts and Purchase Orders
A Panel Discussion

GEORGE C. WATERS, JR., Capt. U.S.N. (Ret.)
Commissioner of Purchase
Nassau County
New York

EUGENE DREXLER
Attorney-at-Law
New York, New York

CAPTAIN WATERS: There seems to be recognition of the need for more and better libraries at the national level with the funds that have been made available through the Library Services and Construction Act. Hopefully, with these funds and the matching funds that will be added to them, and with the emphasis given to library construction and expansion programs by state and local communities, libraries will have a considerably larger sum of money to spend.

Much of this spending will be through contract buying. To digress from the strictly legal aspects of purchasing, we will begin with a general topic, what we call "sophisticated purchasing." That means good, solid purchasing, using public or quasi-public funds, where the director of purchases has control over his purchasing procedures.

One of the important elements in public buying is the matter of competition. Are we really buying competitively? Let us talk about competition—the control of it, the dangers that can be inherent in it, and the values of it.

MR. DREXLER: On the topic of sophisticated purchasing, it is important to understand the word *purchasing*. We are not so concerned about the sophistication of the actual purchase document. The real sophistication comes before the purchase; that is, what is done before a contract is awarded? What is done before an order is placed? That is why we called this session not government contracting or library contracting, but contract purchasing.

Perhaps the first and most important aspect of the sophisticated approach to purchasing is to get as many industry people as possible interested in what you have to buy. You must remember that sometimes you are using public money or quasi-public money. Quasi-public money is part endowment and part public funds. A segment of the public has a right to sell you its products, to take some of that public money. This part of the public that has a right to sell to you, of course, is industry. This is the industry point of view. From your point of view, it is advantageous to have many people in the public who sell, because they are going to create competition, and, thereby, you will receive the best possible price.

We will talk about the lowest price a little later, but, for our purposes, this should be the best price. The best price is obtained by many people competing with each other to sell their goods. In ordinary purchasing you do not care about *creating* competition. Examine your personal spending activity of this morning, or yesterday, or the day before. You will find that you went to someone of your own choice, not necessarily because he had the cheapest scrambled eggs, but because he had the best eggs. You did not care whether the price was thirty-five or forty or fifty cents.

When you spend public funds, however, you must care whether it is thirty-five or forty cents because you are open to criticism if you do not spend the least amount of money. You have a certain amount of money that you can spend, and the cheaper you can buy, the more you can buy. Competitive bidding is probably the most sophisticated way of obtaining a good contract.

CAPTAIN WATERS: It is often said, "We will get competition by going to three bidders." There is really nothing magic about three bidders. If you continue to go to the same three bidders, in a little while you really have no competition at all. To create competition, you need several vendors in the commodities which interest you, and you need to give all of them an opportunity to bid.

In public bidding a purchasing agent is often charged with having favorites when sending out his bids. Having favorites is something that should be avoided. The people who submit requisitions to the purchasing agent often have sources they would like to recommend as possible suppliers. Such recommendations are fine. However, the final selection of sources should generally be left to the purchasing director, the contracting director, or the purchasing agent, whoever is responsible for making the contracts with the vendors and seeing that the proper type of contract is ultimately awarded.

The idea is to develop broad competition, to avoid favoritism, and to maintain control over your vendor sources. If you have a sufficient number of suppliers, vary your selection from the bid list so that you cover it all.

MR. DREXLER: How do you develop this favoritism and not know it? By blindly following the requisitioning people. If you are the purchasing agent, or if you are responsible for the actual purchase, you can rubber-stamp every requisition that comes in. But you will not get the best price or the best quality that way.

You can also create favoritism, for example, by interpreting a part of a bid document to one bidder but not to the others. You have placed that man or company in a favored position by telling him what you want and not telling the others. Perhaps if you had given the others who are competing this same information, the prices might have come down to his level or even lower. You might give one bidder more plans, or more specifications, or more blueprints, or ideas. If you give the same information to the others, perhaps prices will go down and the quality of what you buy will improve.

Favoritism is not only setting one company up as what is commonly referred to as the sole source of a proprietary item or a brand-name item, but it is setting one company up and giving it more information than others about your needs. In this subtle way one company is favored over another. The result is not only criticism, but often a higher price, and perhaps merchandise that is not the best quality.

CAPTAIN WATERS: All of you are probably involved in preparing budgets. In public agencies, budgets are often based on the amount of money spent last year plus some percentage. One procedure that leads to better buying practices is to prepare a shopping list of the items you will require during the coming year. From this list your materials budget can be developed. Later this same list of items serves for the preparation of your requisitions. Following this list, you can set up a purchasing schedule for the whole year whereby your purchase of requisitions can be controlled. You can buy commodities at the specific periods of time when it is best to go into the market, and you can interrelate the budget, the shopping list leading to the budget, and purchasing schedules for the year.

This procedure is a further step in sophistication. Do not just sit back and wait for requisitions to come in and then try to buy on a piecemeal basis. This approach reduces the quantities purchased, adds additional work, and prevents proper scheduling of purchases. If you know at the beginning of the year how you want to set up your budget and what items you want to buy, the purchasing people can handle your requirements more easily.

Get in and work with the budget people early. In my job we are preparing right now for next year. We hope to have our budget and shopping list worked up by the end of this month in anticipation of the '67 budget.

MR. DREXLER: When you think in terms of the large quantities of items needed for the year and of the amount of money you have, you may find there is not enough money to buy what you think you need. Ask yourself, Do I really need this? Or do I really need this expensive quality? Are these my needs, or are these my desires? Is this the kind of pen I really need, or can I accept one less expensive that will perform the same function? If you ask these questions, you can buy more books, or more shelves, or whatever else you really need. Think in terms of reducing your needs to the minimum. Minimum needs of the library will give more for the budget dollar—not more for the money, but more for the budget dollar.

There is a familiar expression, "brand name or equal." The reason "or equal" is used after some specifications for brand-name items is that the law requires it. As a general rule, state laws are written so that purchase cannot be limited to a proprietary or brand-name item; it must be open to "equal" items. Using "brand name or equal" may mean you have not thought out what you really need. You do not need a Westinghouse toaster or equal, you need a toaster. You do not need a Schaeffer pen or equal, you just need a pen. Reduce performance requirements to the minimum necessary to do the job, and you can get away from brand-name procurement.

CAPTAIN WATERS: The best way to get around ordering "brand name or equal" is to have detailed specifications for what is wanted. These specifications can be prepared by the technical people with the assistance of the purchasing people. Specifications for common-use items that are already prepared and available to anyone are those developed by the Defense Department and the General Services Administration. These can be used as the basis for good specifications and then modified for your particular needs.

Sometimes the "brand name or equal" procedure is absolutely essential, when there is no other way to describe what you want. If you do specify your requirements this way, determine in advance how you will evaluate your bids. If salesman X comes in and says, "My brand is this and it is equal to what you have said," how do you determine whether he is right or wrong? If you find yourself in that position, list four or five salient characteristics of the item. You may not care whether it is blue or pink, but you probably do care that it does not extend more than three feet in length and two feet in height, because of space limitations. Do not be concerned about the nonessential characteristics of the item, but remember that certain features may be controlling. If these features are spelled out, you are in a better position to use a "brand name or equal" if you have to.

MR. DREXLER: The brand-name method also sets up a monopoly because very few bidders can really come up with an equal. Chances are you are going to have that brand name come in all the time, thus setting up a nice little monopoly.

DISCUSSION

Comment from the floor: Talking about the use of "brand name or equal" as opposed to that of very detailed specifications, I wonder whether you are not hurting yourself either way.

Years ago we used to specify the Magic Margin feature of the Royal typewriter, for example. If we describe the Royal in great detail, using Royal typewriter specifications, are we not then precluding purchase of IBM or Remington or others? Whereas, if we say, "Royal typewriter or equal," then following your advice, we will judge on the three or four most important aspects. We will accept another item if it does substantially what the Royal typewriter will do. In this way we avoid getting into nuts and bolts and everything else.

CAPTAIN WATERS: A specification prepared by the company is definitely a restrictive specification. One of the things I find unnecessary is to go out on public bid with a restrictive specification, because then only one bidder can supply what I want. You can describe a typewriter not by nuts and bolts but by a performance specification. Performance is another approach to specifications. You can use "brand name or equal," but the most desirable way to buy is to have detailed nut-and-bolt specifications.

Office equipment can sometimes create a problem. I notice that in one of the states—and even in the federal government—all brands of typewriters, for example, are listed in an annual contract. The ordering department can order whatever it wants because neither the state nor federal government has set up a contract and price against which to order. In this case there is no specification problem. It can just order against the contract.

A good, solid competitive specification is the best way to buy; a performance specification is next best; a "brand name or equal" is third in line. A restrictive specification should be avoided at all costs. If you have a restrictive specification so only one type of item or one make of item will serve your purpose, then you are not in a public bid situation. You have led yourself into negotiating with a sole source.

MR. DREXLER: Now I take the role as the lawyer and ask you, "Why Royal or equal?" "Why not IBM or equal?" says IBM. Or why not any other kind of a typewriter or equal? If you say, "Royal or equal," IBM says, "I can't bid the equal of Royal because I haven't got that little gadget you were talking about." But do you really need Royal or IBM, or do you just need a typewriter capable of doing certain things, of a certain size and weight, and appearance and color? If you think of the kind of a typewriter you need, then you can describe your needs in minimum standards. If you think in terms of minimum standards or minimum needs, you can get Royal and IBM to bid.

Comment from the floor: You started off by saying the more you can buy cheaply, the more you can buy. Now, we are breaking this down and discussing the various aspects of a special case, the Royal Magic Margin. IBM has the Selectric. Now, I have made a decision. I want the specific advantages of the Selectric. I also have an admonition from you to the effect that the more I can buy cheaply, the more I can buy. Yet I want one specific feature which is made only by one firm. I am responsible for developing a good operation. To do this, I feel that, even in using public funds, there are certain things I must have to operate effectively. There is no specification that says that public operations must be run inefficiently or ineffectively. We have to take advantage of everything.

I have found that in those cases in which I have taken someone's advice to buy cheaply, we have bought less rather than more because we spent more time replacing. And my time, which has value, is involved in buying and replacing. Very often, cheap equipment is out of commission more frequently than it is in commission. Therefore, I am worried. If I follow your basic statement, I must buy cheaply because this is the best way I can spend the money.

CAPTAIN WATERS: An important concern is economics versus quality. When we talk about buying at the least price, we are not saying to buy at the sacrifice of quality. The minimum specification is that specification which best serves the need. If there is a product below that minimum and this product is bid against your specifications, do not accept it.

On the point of the IBM typewriter with the Selectric head, there are situations in which only this typewriter will serve the need. You must be satisfied if it is your responsibility to select or to buy the one item that will serve a given purpose. In other words, you need a typewriter on which the carriage does not move back and forth, but stays still, and which has an adaptable head that can be changed. This is a patented item, and only IBM sells it. If this is what you need, buy it from IBM.

However, do not make a public advertisement with the Selectric head as part of the specification and expect to get any bids. Then you are really wasting your time and going through a lot of unnecessary paper work. If the Selectric is what you need and you are satisfied that it is, then buy it. In this instance we use negotiation rather than public bidding as a way of buying.

Comment from the floor: As architects, we are concerned with the design of equipment as well as its function. We have found in specifying furniture for public bid that, if we merely specify the performance, we can probably find a hundred chairs that will serve the function, but which will not serve the design. We have been successful in getting competitive bids by specifying the names of three acceptable items by different manufacturers. Then if a contractor wishes to submit other items, we put the burden on the contractor to prove that the item he submits is equal to what we have specified. In that way we control the appearance and the design.

CAPTAIN WATERS: That is a good point. You have developed specifications to the extent you can, but you have used three brand names to set the desired standard of quality. In other words, you have developed a qualified products list, showing only those items which will serve your purpose.

This is another method of buying. To some extent in this discussion, our range of subjects has been too broad and we have aimed at things other than furniture and office equipment, where there is such a wide variety and so many vendors. The basic principle, however, remains the same. Since there will be a lengthy discussion of specifications later, let us say that the best approach to competitive public bidding is to use broad competitive specifications. If this approach does not serve your purpose, move down the line into the other areas we have discussed.

MR. DREXLER: When you are engaged in public purchasing, you must also examine the statutory re-quirements for purchasing. I am sure some of the questions that have arisen on the matter of the lowest bid and public advertising have come up because some lawyer has told you that you have to buy on the open market and from the lowest bidder. You have heard that time after time. It is a standard cry of purchasing people, even in the Defense Department, but it is not necessarily the rule. There are exceptions, and one of them is negotiation.

The first thing you must do is have your lawyer examine your need to advertise publicly. Can you buy in a different fashion? If you do not advertise, can you go to the second lowest bidder or the third lowest bidder, or can you throw out all bids and readvertise? You do not necessarily have to confine yourselves, as public officials, to the offer of the lowest bidder, but you must go to the lowest responsible bidder. Examine the bidder's responsibility.

Check procurement practices with your lawyer. The law may require advertising or it may not. If it does not require it, ask how else you can accomplish your purpose. You do not have to follow the gospel of a buying agent who does not know the law. Check your counsel for that. You may also have to check with your counsel for local ordinances about whether or not you can buy a foreign product, many of which are far superior to American products. You may not be confined to purchasing in your local community as a matter of law, but you may be confined as a matter of politics. As director of the library, you can make the judgment whether you want to follow the politics or not.

The law may, in fact, prohibit the purchase of a brand-name or proprietary item. Check brand-name purchase with your lawyer. If it is prohibited, ask your lawyer to find a way to do what you want to do. This is his job, to find a legal way to get what you need. If you need that special feature on the IBM or on the Royal, then buy it, but find the legal way to do it. The law may require you to include in your ultimate document certain special provisions such as an examination of the record. Check with your lawyer on the legality of how you are buying as well as of the document itself.

One thing which people in government service do not generally realize is that most laws require a written document before a contract can bind the supplier. Many people reach an agreement verbally, on the telephone, but such an agreement may not be an acceptable form of contract. Check this procedure with your lawyer, too. As sophisticated purchasers, check your procedures with a lawyer to see that you are following the law. If you are not satisfied with what your purchasing agent tells you, ask him if it has to be so and where it says so in the law. If he says that he is a lawyer or he says that it is the law, check his advice out with your lawyer if it is still not what you want. There is no reason to believe that the law, or the local ordinances, or regulations will prohibit you from getting the best possible library equipment for your dollars.

You may have to sacrifice the special item on the Remington because if you buy that typewriter you may not have enough money to get an air-conditioning unit. Consider then which you really want, a special item or an air conditioner? Get a cheaper air conditioner or cheaper typewriter, and you satisfy your requirements for that year. But do it because that is your plan or program for a better library. Do not say that the law prohibits you from getting what you need.

Comment from the floor: It is true that most of us abide by the generalizations you have stated, but we find them enormously restrictive for two or three reasons. One, because we do have a type of consumer service available to the libraries now. In many instances we say that we want a specific item and only that specific item because the library world itself has tested this item. However, the business of writing detailed specifications is sometimes enormously difficult.

Secondly, even though we may be willing to go along with what you say about what we want, there is another problem. There are certain vendors we do not want under any circumstances, and excluding those vendors under broad specifications is almost an impossibility. But that is very important to us.

Finally, let me point out that in purchasing there is an intangible which is extremely important. Most large firms are willing to provide prior consultation service—to sit down and plan and organize—if they know they will get the contract. But nobody on an open bid is going to take the time and the expense involved in coming prior to bidding to provide this service. This is an important service that most of us lack at the present moment in open bidding.

MR. DREXLER: Certainly there are vendors you do not want under any circumstances. We would be in a more difficult defense position than we are if we had to buy everything from every vendor. Never in the history of procurement for any federal, state, or local service has one been bound to the lowest bidder. You are never bound to the lowest bidder, but you may be bound to the lowest responsible bidder. That word *responsible* is the vital word which every procurement agency knows, and every lawyer knows. Responsibility is a matter for you to decide.

Is this lowest bidder financially responsible? Can you rely upon him to stay in business to build the piece of equipment you need? Does he have integrity? Does he have the plant capacity, the quality control, the management capability, the technical know-how, the experience, the personnel? Is he overloaded with a backlog of orders? Will he deliver the item when you need it? This is for you to determine. Only when you are arbitrary as determined by a court of law will your purchase be declared void or illegal. Most reviewing agencies will not question your decision that a company is not responsible.

You have to make an examination, however. You have to justify your position because the company you disqualify is going to go to a councilman, or the district attorney, or a state senator, or an assemblyman, or a county executive, or to a senator or a representative in Congress. Be prepared to justify why this man or this company is not responsible to build the item you want. Then you can disregard him and go to the next low bidder.

CAPTAIN WATERS: Remember that you must be able to document your conclusion that a vendor is not responsible. For example, when something which is not good arrives, do the receiving people accept it and do nothing about it, or do they report back to the purchasing point so that there is documentation that the vendor furnished a poor item and that action can be taken to get the proper item?

If this is a competitive vendor, then it is the responsibility of the purchasing people to declare this vendor nonresponsible. But the charge must be documented. I have found cases in which a vendor is the low bidder and the buyer will come in and say, "We don't want to do business with XYZ, because we have had problems in the past." And I say, "Well, what were the problems? Bring out the file and let's see, because we have to have a valid reason to reject the low bidder." Often the file shows nothing, but somebody remembered that in the last three deliveries of XYZ, the material was poor.

Another method we have found helpful in selecting vendors is actually to see what sort of a plant the fellow has and how he makes things. When a vendor bids whom we do not know, and on whom we cannot get a good check, we will send an inspector to make a report.

As a case in point, one vendor who bid on cleaning chemicals was annoyed because he did not get the award. Although we did not think his product was the best, we did not have a good reason to reject his bid. This vendor then went to the highest offices in politics and said, "We are not getting awards in making this particular chemical compound." The next time procurement came around, we decided we could not keep him out. So the vendor bid along with four or five others. Having recently hired an inspector, I said to him, "Go down to the plant and see what this fellow has to offer." The inspector and the buyer went, and what happened? The president of this firm stood at the front door and said, "I will not let you come in. You can't look at my plant. I have trade secrets I don't want you to see." This was nonsense. The fellow did not even have a plant. It was in the back end of a garage. We had no trouble throwing that vendor out as being nonresponsible. But we have the record now and there it is. We will not have any problems with that vendor delivering poor-quality items.

Question from the floor: This is for the attorney on the panel. You were talking about the buildup of a file. We have to build up a file on personnel before we can fire them. We have to have a long file in case anybody comes back and says, "Why did you do this? Why did you do that?" What I want to know is what can be considered a legally justifiable basis for not purchasing? I have three particular problems in mind.

An earlier speaker mentioned the problem of eliminating the unqualified vendor. One of the situations he mentioned is when a person knows a franchise holder who is prime only in the sense that he is making delivery or he has developed an order. On the question of holding the vendor responsible, we have a situation in which a man is the vendor, but he is not responsible for the material. When we find this out later, we have to go back to the factory somewhere else and expect the people there to do something.

Secondly, something new has developed known as the drop shipment. This practice enables the vendor to operate on a very low overhead. What happens if something goes wrong? How do we determine responsibility if the material comes through for many years and then suddenly it does not come through? What recourse do we have and to whom?

Thirdly, is it legitimate to refuse a purchased item for which we requested inside delivery when the trucker refuses to deliver it inside because, "I am alone, I can't carry a thousand pounds," and takes the goods back. The company that sent the material out is reliable; the trucker it hired proves not to be. Is this incident a legitimate basis for not continuing to do business with a company, even though you want its materials?

There are several problems to work out, and I would like to know if it is legally justifiable to use any one of the situations I have described as a basis for not purchasing.

MR. DREXLER: One of the problems may be that your bid document did not include enough restrictions on what you want and where you want it. Learn from your past experience. If you have had difficulties with a franchise holder or with a dealer, then ask in your bid that the name and address of the manufacturer be given. You can also say in your bid, "No subcontracting will be allowed." If the job is a bid by a dealer, then perhaps you will want the dealer and the manufacturer to join in a contract, making both responsible. You can make this stipulation in your bid.

The point is, if you have had these difficulties before, you cannot ask the lawyer or the lawmaker to pass an *ex post facto* law, that is, a law to cover a past failure. A law, or a regulation, or a contract provision, or a bid provision can be made to prevent the same thing from happening again. That is preventive law. As a matter of fact, that is the history of our legal institution. We are a nation of people who have lawmakers to plug up holes as the holes occur. Very few laws are built on a possibility which may happen in the future, except for broad social laws. Even when such laws are made, there are usually loopholes, and someone finds them. Then the lawmakers cover them up. Much the same process applies to bid documents. That is the first thing I see from these three questions you asked.

The question on the drop shipment I will give to Captain Waters, but the third point about the trucker is very interesting. I have the same problem and I am a lawyer. Recently I purchased a couch at Macy's in New York. A trucker came to my door and said the couch was delivered. "I am not going to bring it upstairs in the elevator. I am not paid for that." I said, "I made a deal with Macy's, and if you won't deliver it to my apartment, take it back." He delivered it to my apartment. Let him fight it out with Macy's.

Now, it is not always that easy, I know, to resolve your problem with a thousand pounds of furniture. Get the vendor on the phone and tell him, "Either you get someone here to help this man unload, or I am going to cancel the order for your breach of contract."

You have to use the law in your favor, but watch out. The purchase order may be defective and ambiguous concerning where he is to deliver the goods. Check the purchase order with your lawyer for such aspects as whether delivery shall be FOB at a destination near the plant, or near the site, or in the building, or at the wharf, or at some other particular point. You must know where you want the goods delivered. What is defective in the last point you made is that the purchase order did not say anything about destination. If the purchase order does not say what the parties intended, it is an illegal agreement. So I cannot say whether you should tell the furniture man he is wrong or right.

Comment from the floor: In buying any quantity of furniture, we have found that the best way to handle the situation is to bond the suppliers and, as far as delivery of furniture is concerned, specify that the furniture be set up in place and the refuse removed, because sometimes the problem of refuse from furniture crating is worse than that of having the furniture left on the sidewalk. In all cases in which we have taken bids of this type, we have never had any problems.

CAPTAIN WATERS: This brings us to the subject of performance bonds, a good technique, particularly if you have some doubts about the people you are dealing with. It is the bidder's responsibility to respond under a performance bond.

Concerning the drop shipment situation, I have found some handlers who have an office in their hat and work on a very close margin. Some of them work out fairly well. But I try to get away from buying from the marginal vendor by setting up certain ground rules that he has to meet before we consider him a responsible bidder. In other words, is he recognized as a regular dealer? Is he recognized as a regular distributor? What sort of a contractor arrangement does he have with the various sources that he represents? Do they stand behind him as a drop shipper?

The best approach is to get away from doing business with them at all and deal with a reliable wholesaler or with the manufacturer.

Question from the floor: What about the matter of service? What about the attitude, "I will always buy from company X because we get the best service from him, and his serviceman has the biggest Pepsodent smile"?

CAPTAIN WATERS: This attitude occurs fairly regularly. I find it in my present job. We do tend to buy from a company which gives good service, either the preliminary service of somebody checking things in advance and sitting down and consulting or service after a contract award.

Service, however, is something that can be bought, and bought competitively. Either it can be part of the bid when you are buying the hardware and service is one aspect of the purchase, or it can be handled under a split service contract competi-

tively. There are companies, for example, that sell nothing but typewriter repair service. This is their only endeavor, and they are in competition with the manufacturers of typewriters who also have service organizations. So service can be bought competitively, too. But I agree that it is very difficult to play down service, because service is a part of what we expect when we buy from a responsible vendor.

Sometimes there seems to be a hesitation on the part of the purchasing agent to question with whom he is dealing. This should never be so. Never be hesitant or reticent about asking questions. There are various sources of information on vendors or manufacturers such as the Dun and Bradstreet confidential bank reports or credit-rating bureaus. You can also question the bidder, or you can conduct your own survey of the prospective bidders to determine the sort of companies or persons with whom you are doing business. There are various sources from which you can get information. The point is that the purchasing agent, in dealing with vendors, should be active and aggressive rather than passive. His vendors will respect him more for it.

MR. DREXLER: Never think that anybody in law is going to say that you have no right to find out whether or not the prospective vendor is worthy of selling to you, or, as we phrase it legally, being responsible. You have a responsibility higher than to this vendor. You have a responsibility to the public because it is the public's dollar you are spending, and as a public official or a quasi-public official, whatever position you accord yourselves in that sense, you still are using tax dollars. Therefore, you have more rights than the average person, and you have more duty.

With that duty you can control the people with whom you are dealing. You can go directly to the man or the industry and ask for all the information needed to determine whether or not it is worthy of selling to you. If the vendor refuses to give you this information, you need not, as a general rule, give him the award. You can refuse to give him the award because you cannot determine his responsibility. When he gets the word that you are a "hard buyer," he is going to give you the information you need and will certify it with a CPA audit or affidavit or swear to it under an affidavit if you have doubts about his integrity.

It is easy for me to say, "We will go out and survey," but suppose you are in Chicago and the seller is in Florida. Who is going to survey him? Your counterpart in Florida through this Association [American Library Association] can be your authorized representative to find out, or do a field survey, as some defense people call it. You can use your own people, or hire various services to do it.

A point I have heard mentioned several times is that you have to go to the lowest bidder. No, you do not have to go to the lowest bidder. You go to the lowest responsible bidder, not to the lowest bidder. In fact, you must not go to the lowest bidder if he deviates substantially from what you want. He may deviate either in his response to the bid documents, or by a sample which you think will not meet your specifications, or by what he says he is going to give you when you go out and survey him. You must not make an award to the lowest bidder if he does not respond to every essential aspect of your invitation, including price, quality, and delivery. If he gives you a later delivery than you want, you must reject him. If he gives you an item different—perhaps better—but different, then reject him. If he gives you an item less than what you want, reject him.

This is the truest form of public bidding, to make the award to the lowest responsible, responsive bidder. Not only can you reject a bidder for being nonresponsive, but you can throw the entire bid out and readvertise.

Comment from the floor: I was recently in a position where I had to go to the lowest bidder, although I knew his specifications were defective—that is, the library knew his specifications were defective.

MR. DREXLER: Nothing could be more wrong than that. What you do in such a case is to cancel the whole bid and rebid with amended specifications. It is true that you should not readvertise simply because you do not like the low bidder. This is not a proper, honest way of doing business. Once whole bids or prices are exposed, readvertising simply because you do not like the low man makes a mockery of bidding. But if you think that all the prices are too high, that they are unreasonable, you can, on that basis, readvertise.

Do not think your hands are tied by some very strict law. I said earlier that the law is worthless if it ties your hands. No law or regulation should be so worded that it does not give you discretion. However, the law will stop you if you arbitrarily or capriciously use that discretion to set one man against another, or if you throw all bids out because you do not like the low bidder and ultimately get the man you want or the company you want.

CAPTAIN WATERS: You took the two words that I was about to use, *arbitrary* and *capricious*. I think if the purchasing director would always bear in mind that decisions must never be made in such a fashion, then decisions will be properly made. I have had a number of cases in which awards made other than to the low bidder have been challenged, and the main point I fell back on was that the decision made by the contracting officer or director of purchase was not arbitrary or capricious, but was made on the basis of solid facts, supportable facts.

MR. DREXLER: When we say the lowest bidder and the lowest responsible bidder, it means, please understand, who in your honest discretion is the lowest responsible, responsive bidder. These are classic words of the art, and no lawyer or city attorney is going to tell you differently.

CAPTAIN WATERS: There are really two methods of buying. We have been developing a few thoughts on the first, that is, through formal advertising, or public advertising, or public bidding. You may phrase it differently in your own vernacular, but the phrases all mean the same thing. That is, it is a public bid, it is one in which you expect competition, it is one in which there are nonrestrictive specifications, and it is one in which the persons who do the requisitioning and the people who do the purchasing work together in developing the kind of a bid, or the kind of advertisement, or the kind of solicitation that will get what you want at the best possible price. This is what public bidding really means.

We touched earlier on restrictive specifications when the question came up from the floor. This is a matter that should be stressed, because there is a great tendency for purchasing people to be given restrictive specifications; that is, restrictive to one source. This does not mean that, under certain conditions, you may not want to buy one product, such as the Selectric typewriter or some other patented item, when it is the only one that will serve the purpose. We will talk about them later when we discuss negotiation, but putting restrictive specifications on a public bid is a poor way to do business.

Recently, for example, I ran into a situation in which restrictive specifications had been developed by the requisitioning people for some laboratory equipment. The buyer attempted to loosen these specifications a little bit. We went out on bid and found we had competition for the first time on this type of equipment. The low bid in this procurement was about $68,000 total, and this was $8000 under the second low bid. The basic specifications had been based on a proprietary source. Through modifications which did not in any way lessen the value of the equipment, we were able to get competition for the first time and saved $6000 or $8000 on a $68,000 procurement. This is an example of the buyer and the requisitioning people working together to develop specifications which are nonrestrictive.

Most of our discussion thus far has been about competitive bidding and general purchasing philosophy. The second method of buying, negotiation, is an area in which many people do not become involved except possibly in small purchases such as $200 or $300 items. For some reason, the term *negotiation* has generally had an evil connotation in public buying. This should not be true, but even the press has quoted certain public officials who have denounced negotiation as a method of buying.

Negotiation, under proper conditions, may be one of the best methods of buying. Consider a situation such as we just mentioned where you need a proprietary item and do not want to go to public bid. Instead, you can negotiate with the source supplying this proprietary or patented item and get the best price, the fair and reasonable price. Negotiation is often an excellent way to buy.

MR. DREXLER: The advantage of negotiation is that you can usually get a better price. If you are going to advertise throughout the country, with newspapers and ads, but one company or one man knows he is the only bidder, he is going to give you a high price. You can help matters by letting him know that you are going to examine his bid carefully—question why he is charging this price, how much he is putting in for labor and for material, what labor rates he is using, what contingencies exist, and how he arrives at his price. This examination is what sophisticated purchasing people call cost breakdown. It is really a bill of materials. When you get your car repaired and say, "Give me a breakdown," you usually get an itemized account. An itemized account will help you talk to the company about a fair and reasonable price.

Finally, you may ask whether this is the lowest price the firm charges anyone. This is another tactic to use in negotiation. As a matter of fact, you can even ask it in advertised bids. Ask the bidder to certify that the price he bids is the lowest he charges the same or similar buyers.

The important factor in negotiation is to talk, talk, talk. You talk to the seller and you talk to him about price. Then you talk to him about quality— "What am I getting for my dollar? How do you propose to solve my technical problems? What colors do you propose? What kind of design are you giving us?" In this give-and-take lies the value of negotiation. I know of no law which prohibits negotiation under the circumstances which call for it. Such

circumstances exist when you cannot adequately describe what you want in an advertised bid, when there is no competition for the advertised bid, or when only two or three companies—or one company—are repetitively responding.

Negotiation may be used when you have no past history of pricing on a particular item or when it is a new item for you and you want to test the price structure, the costing that went into it, or the estimate that went into the profit that a man or company is getting. In the latter case, consider 45 or 60 percent profit too high. If you see there is such a profit, start negotiating the price downward.

Remember, negotiation is used not only to get the best price, but it is also a standard method of getting the best supplier, because you are only going to ask the best suppliers to bid. You choose three, four, or five known companies that are qualified, and then you choose the best price submitted by them.

CAPTAIN WATERS: Often the charter for a municipality or a local ordinance or law will be restrictive. It may establish public advertising as the only way to buy or set certain dollar levels above which you can never buy except through public advertising. Perhaps it leaves a few loopholes which require you to go to the city council or to the board of supervisors to get authority to buy other than through public bidding. Such restrictions are common. There is a tendency for local officials and local counsels to shy away from granting a deviation from the old-fashioned formal bid for everything they buy, because it has never been done before. That does not make it wrong, however. It is up to the requisitioning people and the purchasing people to stress the value of this procedure in obtaining the best price for the particular something they are trying to buy.

MR. DREXLER: The procedure can be abused. That is its danger. Too often the pendulum swings to the other side, and the buying agent in government will use negotiation as a technique for setting his cousin up in a contract, or his son-in-law, or friend, or someone he knows. This example shows the abuse of negotiating power. Because of such abuses, negotiation is often avoided. Too often it is only the bad aspects of negotiation to which attention is drawn.

In military procurement, incidentally, a recent survey showed that more than 78 percent of the dollar amount spent for missiles and complex weapons systems was on a negotiated basis. Of the total dollars about 22 percent of the number of procurements, the small ones, was on an advertised basis. Negotiation is a good system for buying as long as it is not abused. If negotiation is the method best suited for a particular kind of procurement, use the law to support your decision.

CAPTAIN WATERS: Negotiation does not mean lack of competition. You can negotiate competitively, particularly when you have insufficient specifications or when you want several companies to compete with technical proposals for design. Then you lead into negotiation of how much it is going to cost to buy the design selected. Also, blanket permission to deviate from public bidding can be granted by the city council, or board of supervisors, or whoever authorizes such.

In other words, if an item you buy repetitively is available from only one source, get an ordinance passed which will permit negotiation for one year, two years, or for all time. Again, however, the purchasing agent has to make sure that he has followed procedure and that his file will so indicate, because all of us in public buying are responsible for doing it the right way and for having an auditable record to support it. Negotiation properly done, with a file properly documented, can never really be questioned.

MR. DREXLER: There are other things you may want to negotiate in addition to price. You may want to negotiate the kind of contract by which you will ultimately abide. We all know the standard, fixed-price contract. This is what we want. Give me a price, and that is it—win, lose, or draw. That is the price you are going to get.

It may be that a fixed-price type of arrangement is bad for the item or service you want. For example, how can you obtain repair services on a fixed-price basis? How do you pay for a repair contract? Or when you advertise or negotiate for repair services, can you say, "Fix all my typewriters for $500 each or $200 each?" No. You will negotiate on what is commonly referred to as a time-and-materials basis. You will ask for competitive time price; that is, how much is the charge for a man-hour of work and all materials at cost. The lowest bidder on a time basis might very well be successful. A time-and-materials contract is usually called T&M.

It may be that you have too many contingencies involved in this type of contract and too many unions. Maybe you will say, "We ought to pay this man for all the costs he has incurred. We will give him a profit." Such an agreement is called a cost contract. The other party to the contract will keep his costs, which will be reviewed by your auditor, or public accountant, or public controller, and he will be paid for all his costs.

But watch out. You may get yourself in a trap when you give him all his costs because he has to make some kind of a profit. He will say, "Okay, give me all my costs and give me 10 percent of my costs for profit." This is called a cost-plus-percentage contract and is improper because the more costs incurred, the higher the profit. There is an incentive for him to be careless and thus increase his costs. To avoid this, ask him beforehand, "How will you estimate your costs for this job?" Then bargain with him on what that estimate will be. Based upon that estimate, take a percentage—3 percent, 5 percent, however you can negotiate—and say, "That will be your fixed fee, a fee for the services you will render us, and no matter how much your costs, whether more or less than that estimate, your fee remains constant." Now he has no incentive to increase costs because even if he does, he is still going to get the same fee. If you discuss that fixed fee with him, he is going to keep his costs down. There is no reason why he should keep his costs up. This is the procedure under the rare circumstance when that kind of contract is needed. I mention it so that you will understand that negotiation can take on a variety of dimensions.

Question from the floor: In regard to what you have just been discussing, are you not really talking about negotiation for services as opposed to negotiation for materials alone? It seems to me that this is a specialized area in which many of us may be becoming more involved.

CAPTAIN WATERS: We would like to emphasize that when you are in a situation in which you cannot come up with sufficient support for a publicly advertised procurement, then the only other way is to negotiate the procurement, whether it is for hardware or for services.

In buying hardware you generally know what you want and are willing to buy from several vendors, or you go out and solicit a technical proposal from several vendors. Then you get a cost proposal for what it would cost to build the unit you want. You may select to negotiate with one, or two, or three, or all of those who respond to this type of solicitation. Or you may negotiate only with those who extend to you the acceptable technical approach and whose costs seem to be within reason. Next, negotiate the cost and the profit. This approach can be used when you do not have specifications, when, in effect, you are buying a proposal which itself becomes the specification for the item you desire.

MR. DREXLER: The end result may be a piece of

very complex electronic gear for use in your libraries. I am certain that as our technology advances, we are going to have more complex equipment installed in libraries. Perhaps it will be similar to an item you learned about in California and which you want in New York. Or you may want an item not quite like it, but a trifle different to meet your own purposes. I am sure that, while this is not historically the equipment librarians buy, it is the kind of equipment which will be bought in the future.

CAPTAIN WATERS: Perhaps you are going to computerize your filing system or card files. You do not necessarily have to advertise for this equipment, and do not let anyone tell you you do. You may have to do a little work on your own by getting the supervisors or council together. But that is your job.

In negotiated and advertised bids, we have not discussed the forms to be used.

MR. DREXLER: The contract forms you will ultimately have to use can be classified by several types. You may use a long form or a short form. For complex equipment you may want to use a long form. For a relatively inexpensive item you may want to use a short form, or for a $100 item you may want to use an open order or purchase order which will not be binding unless and until delivery is accomplished. This is the standard purchase order way of doing business.

If you advertise for bids, you cannot use this type of document. You must have a firm contract which binds both you and the supplier. This contract method is for large procurements. The open order procedure requires no forms at all. You tell the supplier what you want and the date you want it delivered. The day of delivery you pay him. You can cancel any item you want to in most states.

Most long and short contract forms consist of standard clauses, which we call "boiler plate." I cannot tell you now the seventy-five or more different clauses that may be included. However, you should use those clauses, which lawyers call articles, that are required by law or statute. As a matter of fact, if there is federal money involved, you may have to include certain clauses required for federal contracts. We do not know, but your local lawyer can tell you.

For example, it may be that the Controller General of the United States wants the right to examine the books of the supplier because you are using funds over which he has watchdog authority from Congress. He may want to see where that money is going. So you may have to put in a clause which requires "examination of records by the United States Controller." Perhaps the state controller

or the city controller wants the same right. You may have other standard clauses required by law. For this reason you must work directly with your attorney.

But you, too, should think of clauses or articles which will work for you. I can think of several. The prime one is a "changes" clause. You should reserve the right in your contract to make changes in the specifications and to reimburse the contractor or the vendor on an equitable basis. Unless you reserve that right, when you find that you have to make changes, the vendor can refuse to do so. Or he can make them at an extraordinary price increase that will stand up in court. So reserve the right to change the specifications during the course of the contract—the specifications or drawings, whichever term best describes the end item or service you are getting. At the same time, remember the bidder has a right to demand money for such changes. That will be a matter of negotiation between you and him. If you cannot agree, you may want an arbitration clause in your contract. The American Arbitration Association is available for arbitrating disputes between city, state, and local governments and vendors.

Also, you will want to describe in your contract the method of inspection and the criteria for quality control. Thus you can see to it that the man who is delivering to you will have a standard of workmanship and a test against which that standard of workmanship can be measured. It is for your technical people to determine how to test the equipment you are purchasing. If it does not meet that test, it must be rejected. Spell out the criteria for inspection, and do not just do what you do in everyday practice, such as having a suit or dress cleaned. Oddly enough, you inspect then because when you get a suit or dress from the cleaners, you hold it up and perhaps you say, "Hey, that spot didn't come out." This is a visual inspection. You must be more sophisticated in inspecting the tolerances, the degrees, the weight, and the size that go into your specifications. You must have both test criteria and inspection criteria.

You should also specify the time when acceptance takes place, that is, when title passes to you. A contract is usually difficult to interpret when there is a fire in the contractor's plant or when there is a loss in transit from the contractor to you. At such times questions of who is responsible and who will pay arise. As a general rule, you will have to go to court, so state in the contract when acceptance will take place. Remember that after title passes to you, you are responsible for the loss.

You should also include a clause stating who is to pay, when the vendor will get paid, and how he is to bill you. How to bill and when the vendor gets paid can be vital questions. If there is a long lead time before the manufacturer will deliver, he may want to get paid gradually, while he is producing. Such payments are called progress payments. He may want these progress payments, and you may be willing to give him this benefit. If you do agree to make progress payments, however, you should have a lawyer tell him in writing that you want an equitable title or a lien on the goods you are buying while they are in his plant. Or you may want to say that he will get paid not upon progress, but upon delivery.

If he is going to deliver one hundred units over a period of six months, the lawyer's question is, When is delivery? It can be upon receipt of the hundredth unit or on the first month, but since it is unfair to have this man wait for full payment until he delivers the hundredth item, he may be paid in installments. These matters must be worked out with your counsel in a standard form.

Comment from the floor: Here is another suggestion for those who are concerned with buying furniture from the lowest bidder and having it fall apart within a year. Put a guarantee in the contract and be sure that the guarantee is covered in the performance bond. You can put in two years or whatever you think is feasible.

Comment from the floor: I represent a manufacturer and as I listen to what is being said here I am troubled. You tell us that the worst kind of public bidding is that which names manufacturers, yet in the Minneapolis or Midwest areas, because most libraries are relatively small, this is the only economical way of bidding. In other words, to utilize your technique of detailing every single thing you want to buy would require drawings and work that might make the specifications cost as much as the whole furnishings budget.

If you set up the specifications for a new library, you have to include carpeting, draperies, lounge furniture, and occasional furniture, as well as technical furniture such as shelving, card catalogs, etc. If you do not say, "I'd like to buy such and such a chair and/or equal," you will have to provide very detailed drawings and descriptions of what you want to buy. I do not think this is practical. The kind of purchasing you are talking about is for single items. Maybe you can get fifteen manufacturers competing. You can also get competition from the dealers who represent those manufacturers.

CAPTAIN WATERS: The point has been made before that if you get competition among dealers offering the same brand, this is legitimate competition. I also mentioned earlier that a number of basic specifications are available from other agencies which have already developed them. The General Services Administration of the federal government has developed specifications for many of the items you use. To what extent these specifications have been used in libraries, I do not know. But, again, you can select the specification you want for a particular chair or piece of furniture and use the specification as it is or modify it.

I agree that if you are buying a $100 item and you are going to buy only one that year, you buy "brand name or equal." If you buy this way, you must know what characteristics you want. In this case you need not set up a specification, you can say XYZ or equal, but it must be of a certain size, a certain configuration, or a certain color, or it must have other features which are significant to you. These details need be no more than a few sentences added to the "brand name or" specification.

What you do depends on the dollars involved and the complexity of the item. For example, if it is a gun mount or something equally complicated and elaborate, you are going to need specifications. If you are going to buy complicated equipment for the library, you need specifications and drawings to get out a competitive bid. In buying such equipment you may need technical proposals from some companies. But the dollar sign does affect the specifications. If you are going to buy $50 worth of something and you want to buy brand X, there is no restriction requiring you to get competitive bids. Go downtown and buy brand X.

In many cases $1000 is the cutoff point above which you must obtain competitive bids. Anything under that you can buy by some other method, one of which we have been calling negotiation. In that case the need for specifications is not as great, and it does not have to be. The dollar level does have an effect on how deeply you go into specifications, on how widely you seek competitive bids.

Comment from the floor: One of the difficulties in evaluating competitive bids is caused by the statement in the specifications "or equal." For example, I want to buy brand XYZ sofa with a specific type of cover, and after listing the specifications I add the phrase "or equal," which I must do in accordance with the law. Three other bidders are willing to tear their sofas right down to the frame in order to establish that they are equal to my specifications. Unless I do testing, I have no guarantee that sofa ABC is in fact equal to my specifications, and I must rely on the integrity of the manufacturer.

I suggest that any time a bid for a particular piece of furniture is significant that you take the best buy rather than the "or equal." If new libraries are designed as a whole unit by the architect or planning staff, you must take into consideration color, scale, texture, pattern, and other design factors. If you change a chair in relation to a table that you originally had in mind, it could affect the entire design. I do not see how you can ever anticipate everything in your original furniture budget.

In other words, this whole process is very complicated.

MR. DREXLER: Our intent was to show that the purchasing process is complicated and that it requires what we call sophisticated purchasing.

Comment from the floor: I think that in a situation such as you have just described the development of the interior of the library becomes in effect an artistic composition. It has to be looked at this way.

In dealing with architects, you do not have them bid for the job. Their rates are fairly standard, but not entirely so. You choose a man on the basis of his past performance, and you say, "This is the kind of building we want." When you get to the inside, you can ruin a library—absolutely ruin it—by making changes such as were just mentioned. An architect can work up a harmonious design or composition, and then one piece or one group of pieces of the wrong design destroys the whole appearance. You have to leave a good deal to the integrity and the judgment of the people who are creating the effect.

CAPTAIN WATERS: I did not know that you cannot hire architects competitively.

Comment from the floor: Although AIA [American Institute of Architects] suggests standard fees for architectural services, it also provides guidelines for formal architectural competition.

CAPTAIN WATERS: I am looking at it from the government's point of view. I have seen architectural contracts handled on a competitive basis.

I have also seen situations in which the architect recommended the furniture to go in the various offices, and on the basis of his recommendation, we found that we could get competition. I am familiar with one case in which we were talking about $250,000 worth of furniture and the architect on this particular building brought in an interior decorator. The interior decorator, in designing the various offices and equipping them, developed specifications for a competitive purchase of about $250,000 worth of

furniture. The point that was raised throughout was that this furniture had to meet a certain quality level, and we specified the quality level. We did not develop detailed specifications. We did specify that any one of three manufacturers' products would be acceptable. In this way competition was obtained. Each situation must be faced as it comes. I think that architectural contracts as well as furniture buying can be obtained competitively.

If you start from scratch, as pointed out here, and hire someone to do your total planning and equipping for you, this is another approach. The agency representing the government should retain control over what is going on, even to the extent of approving the subcontractors with whom the prime contractor is going to do business and approving the bids or quotes the prime contractor receives from the subcontractor. This control you are entitled to keep when you are buying and representing the government in spending public or quasi-public funds.

Question from the floor: How do you legalize a contract? Whose signature is binding?

MR. DREXLER: The local, state, or municipal ordinances will tell you which persons in local authority can bind the library. The charter of origin or certificate of incorporation will indicate who has that power.

As a matter of fact, in the federal government there is only one contracting officer who can sign and bind the government to a contract. Oddly enough, I do not know if the President of the United States is a contracting officer and capable of binding the United States government to a contract. It must be a duly appointed, duly designated contracting officer under the law or under your charter who can bind you.

CAPTAIN WATERS: As a further note on that, in my present situation, under the charter I am empowered to contract without dollar limit with only certain limited specifications from the board of supervisors. I, in turn, delegate to my deputies limited contracting authority. This practice is general in most municipalities. It is in the city of New York, and perhaps in other institutions and localities.

Question from the floor: I would like to raise a question regarding deviations or modifications from the specifications. Sometimes you want a certain kind of steel bracing on the stacks—possibly welded as opposed to bolted—or you may want a certain finish, or certain gauge steel, or certain underbracing in the tables. The specification is put in. Sometimes the bidders submit drawings, sometimes they submit photographs; other times they may not. The question I would like to ask is this: Is it reasonable in bid documents to require bidders to indicate when they have modifications?

Modifications can make quite a difference in the actual bid, and you may accept what looks like a low bid. Of course, you do have legal recourse later, but is it generally better to require bidders to indicate the modifications they are submitting? Is the burden on the customer or on the bidder to indicate the deviation from the specification?

MR. DREXLER: First, when a man responds to a bid and states that his item meets the bid, and when by operation of law you say that the specifications govern, it is his responsibility to tell you in what respect his product deviates from your specifications. If he has stated it in such a way that it is not obvious to you that it is a deviation, he has fooled you, although he is bound to the specifications. On the other hand, if he points it out clearly to you, you cannot get him to law. In effect, he is giving you a counter offer, although that may not be a legally binding instrument later on. It may be difficult to administer such a contract. It seems to me that if you have a problem like that, you should say in your bid that unless otherwise indicated the specifications shall govern. No matter what he comes in with, he must abide by the specifications.

Question from the floor: What about insurance? Who assumes the insurance? For instance, if you buy from a local jobber, that jobber has to send to the factory. Does the factory assume the insurance, say for $5000 worth of furniture, or does the local jobber? In case of damage, who takes care of it?

MR. DREXLER: First of all, do you want insurance? If you want it, you pay for it. If you do not want insurance, then you do not pay for it. If the trucker wants insurance to insure himself against liability to you, he will take insurance out on his own. You must determine whether or not you want insurance and whether or not you want to pay for it.

Question from the floor: If the equipment or furniture is damaged in transit, what recourse is there?

MR. DREXLER: That is why I mentioned earlier the importance of establishing when title passes to you in your purchase order or in your contract. If you own the property while it is in transit, you are responsible. If you do not own the property, if you own it only upon delivery to you, then the shipper or the seller is responsible. The contract will determine when you own the property. This is a very fine legal point, and I might add that this question of risk in transit has taken up volumes of books in a law library.

Preparation of Bidding Documents for Library Furnishings and Equipment

FRAZER G. POOLE
Director, Library
University of Illinois, Chicago Circle
Chicago, Illinois

Any librarian who has searched for information on the preparation of contract documents for library furnishings and equipment has been surprised to find that this subject is scarcely mentioned in the library literature and treated only in the most cursory fashion in the literature of purchasing or business management. Indeed, one suspects that this aspect of purchasing procedures is passed from one practitioner to another as were medieval crafts.

In consequence, this discussion is based upon personal experience and upon the experience of librarians and purchasing agents who, of necessity, have prepared or reviewed bidding documents for library furnishings. I am grateful to the several librarians who have shared their experiences with me, as well as to those who have sent me copies of the bidding documents used in furnishing their libraries. I am likewise indebted to those manufacturers of library furnishings who offered suggestions based upon their experiences with the bidding problems of library furnishings.

Some aspects of bidding procedures are subject to varying opinions and to different legal requirements. For some problems there is no one accepted solution. Where possible, both points of view are discussed.

One can hardly suggest that the furnishings of a library are more important than the building. Yet, there is general agreement that the best of new buildings can be enhanced by properly selected furnishings, or that much of the effect created by the architect can be lost if library furnishings are not appropriate in design and in quality. Furniture that does not withstand the rigorous treatment it receives by library users, bookstacks with finishes that abrade too rapidly or with shelves that will not support the loads to which they are subjected, table legs that soon come loose, upholstery that pulls away from the frame, desks with drawers that do not slide properly—these and others are defects that reduce efficiency and add to the cost of library management. Thus, problems affecting the efficient procurement of library furnishings are of special concern to the librarian responsible for modernizing an old building or equipping a new building.

Disappointing—often critical—delays, rebidding, wasted funds, inappropriately designed or badly constructed furniture, even lawsuits may result from poorly written purchase or contract documents. Ordinarily, these problems do not receive wide publicity, but they are perhaps more common than is realized. They happen to large institutions as well as to small.

This discussion of the documents required for the purchase of library furnishings and equipment is based primarily upon procedures used in taking competitive bids. Competitive bidding is nearly always used where tax funds are involved, and the procedure is of interest therefore both to public libraries and to academic libraries which operate under state, county, or municipal control. Competitive bidding is less frequently employed by private institutions, although here, too, it is frequently used if the purchase is of appreciable cost. Even where competitive bidding is not used, detailed specifications are often desirable in order to ensure that the products furnished on the contract are of the requisite quality and design.

In situations in which competitive bids are required by statute, they are also used for routine purchases if the cost exceeds some minimum figure, as well as for those special situations in which substantial quantities of new items are required on a one-time basis; for example, in furnishing a new library. Even when not required by law, the cost of furnishings for a new building will almost always be such as to suggest the desirability of taking competitive bids.

It should be emphasized that competitive bids are taken to ensure (1) the purchase of required items in the appropriate quality at the lowest possible price, and (2) the distribution of public money on a wide basis rather than to the favored few. Competitive bidding does not imply, however, that a contract will be awarded to the lowest bidder, although there is always a presumption that this will be the case. For the purchaser, competitive bidding provides a means of analyzing and judging generally comparable merchandise on the basis of quality as well as of cost.

The above statement is probably more true in theory than in practice, and I am sure many librarians have been involved in situations in which only the lowest bid has been considered, regardless of the quality of the product offered. There is no good solution to such situations, although it is often a matter of educating the purchasing agent or other responsible official on the need for a given level of performance. It also helps if the librarian is prepared to offer assistance in writing specifications that will assure the needed quality.

In actual practice some bid documents are precise and detailed; others are abbreviated and loosely written. Nor is there a wholly accepted terminology for contract documents. In some instances the word *specifications* is used, either alone or as part of a longer phrase, to designate the entire package of bidding or contract documents related to a single job. Properly, however, the term *specifications* is restricted to those portions of the documents that describe in detail the specific characteristics of the furnishings or equipment to be supplied.

Rarely, a library may be successful in obtaining the furnishings it needs without going to the trouble of preparing detailed bidding documents; but when this happens, it is a matter of luck. In most cases problems with vendors, misunderstanding of the library's requirements, the purchase of unsatisfactory furniture and equipment, and the legal difficulties that not infrequently follow are directly attributable to the lack of proper bidding documents and, in particular, to improperly written General Conditions and poorly prepared specifications.

Colleges, universities, and schools with purchasing agents normally place responsibility for the preparation of contract documents on these officers. In a municipality it is usually the city purchasing agent who prepares bid documents. In some instances the architect or designer prepares the documents, or he may be called upon to assist the purchasing agent. In other instances the task will be divided, with the purchasing agent assuming responsibility for those aspects of the documents that must follow a prescribed legal pattern and the architect preparing the technical portions or specifications.

In either case the librarian or library consultant, or both, may be asked for comments, or he may, if qualified to do so, actually write portions of the specifications. Even if the librarian is not qualified to assist in writing the specifications for library furnishings, he ought to be sufficiently knowledgeable to review these documents intelligently and to make suggestions for their improvement.

Both the number and the form of contract documents vary widely, depending upon the experience of the persons responsible for their preparation, the general nature of the furnishings involved, the applicable legal requirements, and whether the furnishings are part of a larger contract.

PRINCIPAL PARTS OF THE CONTRACT DOCUMENT

Generally, a complete set of the contract document will include the following materials, which are here organized into seven principal sections. This is not the only way in which this material can be arranged, but it does follow a generally established and logical pattern. The arrangement used here provides for most variations necessitated by local laws and practices.

Invitation to Bid. This section of the document, also called Notice to Bidders or Bidding Instructions, usually takes the form of a letter in which notice is given to potential suppliers that bids will be taken for specified items or a class of items. The title Invitation to Bid is more appropriate, however, and, since it avoids confusion with the section Instruction to Bidders, is to be preferred. The invitation should provide at least the following information:

> Place and time of bid opening
> Name of item or class of items involved
> Name and address of individual from whom bid documents may be obtained
> Amount of deposit required for a set of bid documents
> Cost of additional sets of documents
> Conditions governing refund of the bidder's deposit.

Also, included, where applicable, may be such information as the following:

> Data pertaining to submission of samples—if these are to be required prior to opening of bids
> Notice of publication of bidding information in newspapers or other media.

Usually, this notice is mailed separately to those suppliers from whom bids are particularly desired. Later, it may be bound with the other bid documents even though distributed previously.

Index. If the bid documents are voluminous, an index is convenient for the user. Shorter documents may not require an index.

Instructions to Bidders. This section of the contract document provides information covering the legal and practical matters relating to the bids. Not infrequently the section designated Instructions to Bidders is confused with that known as the General Conditions. Sometimes the Instructions are included and the General Conditions omitted, or vice versa. Normally, however, both are used. Occasionally, in two sets of documents containing both sections, some of the information in the Instructions in one document will be included in the Conditions in the other. Despite the variation in practice, there is a fairly clear distinction in the purposes of the two sections and it is better if the titles are not used interchangeably.

To repeat, Instructions to Bidders is used to inform potential suppliers about the legal aspects of the bid, bidding procedures, the general qualifications of bidders, the list of documents which make up the contract, and similar matters.

General Conditions. This section of the contract document relates more specifically to the job in hand and provides information about such items as the use of materials other than those required in the specifications, the owner's right to terminate the contract if the supplier fails to conduct the work properly, the conditions under which the contractor may stop work, the general requirements for shop drawings, the owner's right to do work on the premises, indemnity agreements, liability insurance, guarantees to be furnished by the contractor, payment of royalties and fees, the need for compliance with applicable statutes—such as wage and hour laws, state and local purchasing acts—and similar matters.

Not infrequently the General Conditions will be those used by the institution for its building contracts, modified for the furnishings contract. This, however, is a dubious practice at best and sometimes results in contract documents in which the requirements set forth in the Instructions to Bidders are in contradiction to the General Conditions because the latter section was not properly adapted to a new situation.

It is hardly the task of the librarian to reconcile such differences or to suggest the makeup of these sections of the contract documents. Nevertheless, insofar as he is qualified and can afford the time to review these materials, he may be able to prevent serious problems from arising at a later date. Clearly, he can assist here only to the extent that he and his purchasing agent are able to work together cooperatively and effectively.

We do not have space in this paper to discuss all of the elements which make up the General Conditions, but the importance of requiring shop drawings for those items which vary in any degree from standard design or construction should be emphasized. Although this requirement is customary practice, it is not always followed, and more than one instance of the delivery of the wrong item or of an item that does not function properly is traceable to the fact that the manufacturer or supplier was not required to submit shop drawings. Again, the librarian has the ultimate responsibility for his building. The more active and knowledgeable his interest, the better the building will be. Occasionally, a section designated Special Conditions is used. This is applicable where the General Conditions have been originally developed for a different job—for example, for a building contract—and it is desirable to indicate certain special requirements of the furniture installation, such as delivery schedules, installation dates, storage facilities at the site, or refinishing of items damaged during installation. Usually, however, it is preferable to include this information in the General Conditions.

Standard Forms and Agreements. No two sets of contract documents ever contain the standard forms in the same place. The makeup of such forms, of course, as well as the number, will vary, depending upon applicable legal requirements. Typically, these forms and agreements (which preferably should constitute a separate section of the documents) include: an owner's protective bond (also called a performance bond) to be submitted by the contractor and his surety; a materials performance bond, an Agreement form to be signed by the contractor and the purchaser or owner; and various releases and waivers of lien for both the contractor and his subcontractors, together with any other forms required by law. These several forms, when properly completed and endorsed, constitute the legal basis for the agreement between supplier and purchaser.

Miscellaneous Items. Following the above, there are usually a number of other sections, including a list of approved wage scales, lists of approved surety and fire insurance companies, as well as addenda, if any, to the General Conditions. These several sections form both the legal and the general basis for the contract, and the librarian should be aware of their nature and their importance.

Furnishings Requirements by Bid Group. Finally we come to those aspects of the contract document that relate directly to the furnishings of the library and are, therefore, of the most significance to the librarian.

When all furnishings for a new library are to be purchased at the same time, it is desirable to divide them into several reasonably homogeneous groups. This division greatly simplifies the taking of bids, as compared with issuing specifications for a single mixed group of furnishings. In most instances bids are taken on all groups at the same time. The advantage to the owner, in bidding all groups simultaneously, as opposed to bidding each group separately, is that some bidders will bid two or more groups at a reduction in cost over the total cost of separate bids.

The categories used for bidding vary according to the size and complexity of the building, but the following segregates the usual items of library furnishings into groups that may be bid satisfactorily under most circumstances:

Group A. Library steel bookstacks and accessories

Group B. Library technical furniture—wood (circulation desks—if not part of the building contract, card catalog cabinets, book trucks, reading tables, study carrels and tables, chairs, etc.)

Group C. Standard office furniture and equipment

Group D. Lounge and upholstered furniture (occasional furniture, tables, and chairs)

Group E. Carpets and draperies.

Occasionally, it may be desirable to subdivide the above groups. Thus, under some conditions bids may be taken on carpets and draperies separately, or upholstered items may be bid separately from other items of occasional furniture. Again, certain items of office furniture, if desired in wood, may be bid with the technical library furniture, or office furniture may be divided into two sections if composed of both wood and steel items.

The important point is that furnishings should be divided into groups which bidders can bid in their entirety. Many bid complications arise because some bidders cannot supply all of the items called for in a particular group. Carpeting, as an extreme example, should never be included in the same bid group with steel office furniture.

When all bid groups are to be put "on the street," they are usually made up as a single package, with the general sections of the documents bound with those sections that pertain directly to the several groups of furnishings. An alternate procedure is to issue the general sections bound as a unit and to issue separately, upon request of the potential suppliers, those sections relating specifically to the furnishings. In either case each section pertaining to a separate group of furnishings should normally consist of the following: Part I. Detailed Specifications and Part 2. Schedule of Equipment.

Part 1, Detailed Specifications, is required for items to be especially designed or with features that make them different from stock items. In specifying furnishings for which only a catalog number is to be shown—as is often the case, for example, with steel office furniture—detailed specifications are sometimes omitted. Even here, however, it is much better practice to include essential specifications. For office furniture such details include those features necessary to define the level of quality desired, e.g., the locking arrangement on desk drawers, the type of suspension to be used on file and desk drawers, fabric types and colors, material for tops, etc.

Specification in this section of those features considered essential in the furnishings is a means of defining the desired level of quality and provides added assurance of obtaining that quality in those instances in which performance specifications cannot be used. In addition, it is better to include here such items as color of finish and upholstery and the color and type of material for desk tops than to show them only on the drawings, as is sometimes done.

The lack of a standard arrangement for contract documents, the manner in which they are sometimes put together, and the number of addenda required to correct mistakes in the original documents are among the common causes of problems in competitive bidding. Documents which are poorly written and difficult to interpret occasionally discourage suppliers from submitting bids. Listing page after page of items of office furniture in the schedule of equipment while the color, upholstery, and top material are detailed only on the blueprints—thus requiring the estimator in the manufacturer's office to work back and forth from floor plans to specifications in order to establish a list of the number of items in each color—is one way to lose a potential bidder. Coordinating such details is more easily and quickly done when the documents are being prepared by the purchasing agent or architect. Even less defensible is the situation in which the documents contain no schedule of equipment and the supplier is forced to make his own list before he can prepare his bid.

It should be emphasized that many of the problems encountered in the award of bids are traceable to improperly prepared documents. A detailed, accurate, complete set of contract documents is well worth the effort required.

The Detailed Specifications section normally consists of:

> A general paragraph(s) explaining the coding system, defining the type of items required, stating the scope of the work required for the group, and providing any other general or background information pertaining to the bid group involved
>
> A paragraph listing the items of furniture required as samples. For samples representing stock items, the requirements should include delivery twenty-four hours before bid opening and retention of the successful bidder's samples to be used as controls until completion of the job
>
> Paragraphs setting forth requirements for materials, hardware, workmanship, and installation; requirements for shop drawings; performance requirements (both structural and finish); testing to be conducted; samples of finished wood or steel to be tested for compliance with performance requirements; cleanup; and a guarantee statement.

Not all of these subjects must be covered for each bid group, although those mentioned will ordinarily be needed for bookstacks and technical library furniture.

Part 2, Schedule of Equipment, is required for all groups including carpets and draperies. The schedule should include:

> Code numbers of all items as used on the floor plans
>
> Catalog numbers of the items (if the "or equal" procedure is used)
>
> Quantity of each item (the determination of quantities is the responsibility of the owner) and
>
> Description of the item, including all dimensions and other essential features.

COROLLARY DOCUMENTS

The seven sections, beginning with the Invitation to Bid on page 26 and concluding with the Furnishings Requirements by Bid Groups, constitute the principal contract documents. With these, several corollary or supporting documents are usually required. The latter include one or more sets of floor plans with all items of furniture shown in their proper positions and coded to the Schedule of Equipment and sketches of all special equipment or of equipment that differs in any way from standard items selected from a catalog.

The "Or Equal" Procedure. In preparing specifications for furnishings and equipment, two general methods are used: (1) "or equal" and (2) performance and testing. The first is used in situations in which it may be desirable to accept standard items listed and described in a supplier's catalog and identified by a specific catalog number. In other instances the architect and owner may elect to provide custom-designed furnishings. Then, performance specifications, including drawings, will be required.

Where standard items are to be used, the librarian—or other person responsible for preparing the order—is faced with the task of knowing all the principal characteristics of the items he wishes to order. In competitive bidding it is usually necessary to use the term "or equal" as an indication of the buyer's willingness to accept comparable products of other firms.

Despite the fact that the "or equal" clause is often required by law, it is often an unsatisfactory method of procurement. The very term "or equal" is abstract and has little significance when used without qualification. Since the evaluation of quality and performance in such situations is often made on the basis of personal opinion, potential bidders, when attempting to relate "or equal" to cost, are forced to guess who it is that will make the final decision. In some instances the General Conditions state that wherever the term "or equal" (or "or approved equal") is used, the decision is to be made by the architect, the interior decorator, the consultant, the owner, or some combination of these individuals. Although not a universally acceptable solution, identification of the person responsible for the decision does make it possible to use the "or equal" procedure with less fear of later complications. Where such an escape clause is used, it should be carefully worded. The following is an example of suitable phrasing for this situation:

> "Where any article or thing in these documents is specified by a proprietary name, a trade name, or the name of a manufacturer, with the addition of the expression 'or equal,' it is understood: (1) that the architect, (or interior designer, or consultant) acting as the owner's representative, will use his own judgment in determining whether or not any article proposed as an alternate is the equal of any article specified herein; (2) that the decision of the architect on all such questions of equality shall be final; and (3) that in the event of any adverse decision by the architect, acting as the owner's representative, no claim of any sort shall be made or allowed against the architect or the owner by the manufacturer, jobber, or other supplier of the articles involved."

Where the phrase "or equal" is used, a further modification is often helpful. This procedure, which requires the catalog number of at least three different suppliers (the minimum number normally required in competitive bidding) followed by the phrase "as manufactured by the XYZ Corporation," establishes the general level of quality desired more precisely than citation of a single product and makes it more difficult for a supplier to bid on articles of substandard quality. However, the individual responsible for preparing the specifications must know the product lines of more than one firm. This procedure also requires that the term "as manufactured by" be defined in the General Conditions. A suitable statement for such use is as follows:

> "Wherever, in these contract documents, any material, or any item of equipment is defined by describing a proprietary product or by using the statement 'as manufactured by,' it is the intent of the owner that this shall describe the quality of material to be used, the quality of craftsmanship desired, the method of manufacture, and the dimensions. This procedure is not intended to limit bidding to such items, but rather to establish, by reference to acceptable existing products, a standard of quality to which the items furnished on this contract must conform."

Performance Specifications and Testing. The alternative to specifying a proprietary article, and nearly always the only really satisfactory procedure when possible, is to prepare performance specifications for each product involved. Performance specifications differ from the typical nuts-and-bolts specifications so frequently used in specifying library furnishings in that they are based upon the actual performance expected of the article. In other words, the important consideration is how well the product performs, not how it is made. The librarian who requires an installation of bookstacks should be concerned with how this equipment supports books, not with the method of assembly, the gauge of steel, or the dimensions of the supporting columns.

One of the original charges to the Library Technology Program of the American Library Association was to develop standards and specifications for library furnishings and equipment. Studies in this project showed clearly (what industry generally had known for years) that the only way to obtain a given level of quality in the purchase of library furnishings was to develop specifications based upon actual performance rather than upon the materials and methods of manufacture. Yet, desirable though they may be, such specifications have proved extraordinarily difficult to produce.

For many years, and this is largely true today, the majority of specifications for library furnishings have specified only the methods and materials to be used in their production. Since such specifications are usually the standard of a particular manufacturer, they point directly to one product, with the result that other manufacturers are often unable to bid or must submit a qualified bid which is then subject to rejection by the owner.

In too many instances the manufacturer's specifications emphasize special features which may be standard with one firm but require special tooling and dies or costly changes in production methods of others. Requesting such specifications results in increased costs or may simply reduce bidders to an unacceptably low number. Sometimes special features are actually required, but they should not be included in the specifications unless they are.

It was the need for specifications based upon performance, rather than upon methods and materials, that led the Library Technology Program to spend nearly six years in an effort to develop performance standards for library bookbinding. LTP has also done some work on performance specifications for bracket-type bookstacks. Hopefully the Program will be able to develop performance specifications for other items of library furnishings as well.

Wood furniture poses a much more difficult problem in the development of performance specifications than do steel bookstacks. The only approach to such specifications at this time is a series of tests for the durability of the finish. However, such tests provide at least an indirect measure of the general quality of furniture. It is characteristic of the wood furniture business that finishing operations are the most costly element of the entire manufacturing process. No manufacturer of poor-quality merchandise can afford an expensive finish, and no manufacturer of first-line quality dares risk a poor finish. It is logical to assume, therefore, that if the finish is good, the design and construction will be generally satisfactory. For this reason no buyer of library furniture interested in a quality product should fail to include in his specifications a detailed set of tests for finish.

Normally, the stated requirements for such tests as well as the tests themselves should be incorporated in the Detailed Specifications for the group of furniture under consideration. Occasionally, specifications will call only for certification by the manufacturer that his product will pass the tests, but this is not always an adequate safeguard. To ensure compliance, the owner should require finish samples in advance of the bid opening and should have these samples tested by a competent laboratory. Award of the contract should then be contingent, other factors being equal, upon the degree to which the bidder's samples have passed the specified tests.

Nothing said above, however, should be construed to mean that is unnecessary to spell out in detail the requirements for such aspects of furniture as gluing, drying of wood used in construction, methods of fastening, etc. On wood furniture, tests for finish are useful in separating generally good-quality furniture from poor-quality furniture. In the absence of tested performance specifications covering basic design and construction, however, the nuts-and-bolts type of specifications is still necessary.

Coding Furnishings on Blueprints. When furnishings for a new building are involved, it is desirable practice, again not always followed, to prepare floor plans showing each item of furniture in its proper position. All items shown should be identified with code numbers keyed to the various equipment schedules in the bid documents. Some architects and planners prefer to show the complete schedule of equipment on the blueprint. This method has some advantages, but it should not be a substitute for the listing in the Schedule of Equipment. In any case, the coding system should be consistent and as simple as possible. It is good practice to make the first unit of the code number correspond to the letter or number which designates the bid group.

Responsibility for Quantities. The problem of whether the manufacturer or the owner should be responsible for identifying and counting the number of items in each category is a matter of disagreement among specification writers. Some insist that the specifications be so written as to make the manufacturer or supplier responsible for the count; others believe that the owner should specify quantities. The rationale behind the first procedure is that the supplier can be held responsible for any mistakes he makes. Thus, if at final delivery the manufacturer is short two tables, or ten stacks, or three map cases, it is his obligation to supply these items. The other argument states that the owner is in the best position to know the quantities involved and that it too frequently leads to complications in bidding, as well as in final delivery, to leave the matter of quantities to the manufacturer. In practice, even with an expert preparing the specifications, code numbers become transposed, one number is made to look like another, units immediately next to each other in the drawings are misconstrued, and, in the end, the bidder quotes on the wrong quantity. Thus, although the argument that the owner can always hold the supplier responsible sounds logical, experience shows that better and more uniform bids are likely to result if the owner specifies the quantities.

Requirement of Unit Prices by Bidder. Competitive bidding requires, as a matter of course, that the bidder state a total sum for furnishing the articles included in any one bid group. It is also good practice to require that the bidder provide unit prices for all items of furniture "delivered, uncrated, and set in place."

Provision for Adjustment of Quantities. In some situations it may also be desirable to be able to purchase additional quantities of a given item during the period of the contract or for some stated period thereafter. When this is the case, a requirement that the bidder furnish unit prices on the basis of an increase or decrease in the quantity not to exceed some given percentage may be included. Often this is 10 percent of the total bid for the group, but it may be more or less.

Guarantee Period. Contracts should provide a stated guarantee period, although this will differ with the type of product. For this reason, if the bid documents are issued as a package, each group requires a different guarantee period and this normally is a part of the detailed specifications. On the other hand, if each group is bid separately, the guarantee statement may be included in the General Conditions. Guarantee periods in general effect at this time are as follows:

Group A. Library steel bookstacks—5 years
Group B. Library technical furniture (wood)—3 years; except upholstery—2 years
Group C. Standard office furniture—5 years
Group D. Lounge and upholstered furniture construction—5 years; upholstery—2 years
Group E. Carpeting—3 years; draperies—3 years.

Shop Drawings. Wherever items of furnishings are of special design, the owner should call for shop drawings. Ordinarily, the general requirement that shop drawings must be provided will be stated in the General Conditions. Specific requirements for shop drawings should be repeated in the Detailed Specifications covering each group.

Many errors in the interpretation of blueprints and design sketches will be revealed in shop drawings. These should, of course, be examined by the architect or designer *and* by the librarian. Only experience will indicate the several kinds of mistakes that can occur, but a major problem area is in dimensions. Whether the shop drawings are for stacks or furniture, the librarian should check all dimensions on them with the greatest care.

Bidder Qualifications. The problem here, of course, is how to restrict bidding to manufacturers who are fully qualified, without being illegal and without eliminating those who may be qualified but not well known. There is no easy answer to this difficulty. The proper use of performance specifications serves in instances where engineering or laboratory tests can be conducted on the products involved. In some instances such tests may not be feasible. Where this is the case, other criteria may be used to determine the qualifications of the bidders.

Those most frequently used for library furniture and technical equipment are the following:

The manufacturer must have produced items of the type required by the specifications for at least five years.

The manufacturer must have published a catalog of his products for at least five years.

The manufacturer must be able to furnish the names of at least three installations, of equal or greater magnitude than that required in the installation for which he is bidding, made within the past five years.

The ostensible manufacturer of the furniture must be in fact the manufacturer of some major portion of the items required. (In any case the bidder is usually required to list the name and location of the factory where the furniture will be manufactured.)

Obviously, the purpose of such restrictions is to eliminate those bidders who are unqualified by virtue of their lack of experience, inadequately equipped plants, or production of cheap and poorly made products. In some cases these criteria may be too restrictive. A given manufacturer, for example, may have been in the field for several years but only lately issued a catalog of his products. He will not be able to meet the requirements of a "catalog for five years." Yet his products may be generally acceptable otherwise. In general, however, these criteria are reasonable and serve their purpose. If they are used, they must be followed or legal complications may result. In one recent instance a large contract was to be awarded to a firm which, although the low bidder, failed to meet one of the established criteria. One bidder, who had met the criteria but was high bid, objected and threatened to take the matter to higher authority. The result was nearly disastrous.

This matter warrants emphasis. To avoid problems, sometimes serious problems, the owner must be scrupulously honest and fair in awarding contracts. Bidders who cannot meet established qualifications or who do not meet specifications should be disqualified.

When all bidders submit qualified bids, the situation will be complicated, but it is far less likely to cause trouble than if a firm which does not meet the requirements is selected for award of a contract. If the owner cannot properly evaluate qualified bids, then an outside expert should be called in.

Omissions in Specifications and Drawings. There are frequent instances in which items are omitted in either the drawings or the specifications. Unless the owner is protected by special phrasing, he may "lose" such items. It is, therefore, desirable to include in the "general" paragraph of the Detailed Specifications a sentence similar to the following: "Items shown in the drawings and coded to the specifications, or referred to and required in the specifications but not shown on the drawings, shall be furnished just as though fully covered by both drawings and specifications."

Samples. Samples of several kinds may be required depending upon whether stock or special design items are specified. It is usually unnecessary, for example, to require samples of steel office furniture. These products are nearly always uniform in quality within the same line and may be inspected in any office furniture store.

Library technical furniture of wood, on the other hand, is less well known. Further, it is often difficult to find showrooms where representative items can be examined except in major cities, and there is less uniformity of quality in general. Thus, when specifying from the catalog, it may be advantageous to inspect representative pieces prior to awarding the contract. In such instances samples of tables, chairs, card catalog cabinets, and book trucks may be called for. To avoid complications, it is important that such samples be delivered before the date of bid opening. Practice varies, but it is usually wise to specify that such samples be delivered at least twenty-four hours prior to the opening of bids.

At the same time, it should be noted that the preparation and shipping of samples may be a serious inconvenience to the manufacturer and can result in increased costs to the consumer. If the bidders can be prequalified (and this is not possible in all situations) so that bidding can be restricted to those bidders whose products are known to be satisfactory, then samples are seldom necessary and only tend to add one more complexity to the bidding situation. When bidders cannot be prequalified, there is more justification for requiring samples.

Samples of non-stock items, that is to say items to be custom designed, may also be required, but these should be preproduction samples, required only of the successful bidder. There are instances in which custom-designed samples have been required prior to the opening of bids. This is nearly always an unreason-able requirement and may be—in fact, has been—cause for a serious reduction in the number of bidders. Where preproduction samples are required, the specifications should make clear that the cost of such samples is to be added to the total cost and that they will become the sole property of the owner.

The requirement of preproduction samples applies primarily to furniture on which it is impossible to conduct satisfactory tests for performance. It does not apply to steel bookstacks if on-site or laboratory testing is planned. For testing, samples should be required for delivery prior to the opening of bids. Tests may be conducted before or after bid opening. Samples of the successful bidder should be retained as controls against which to measure stacks delivered to the job. Test panels of finished metal and wood will also be required if laboratory testing is to be conducted. The requirements of such test panels should be carefully spelled out in the specifications covering the items in question.

Sketches. Sketches are clearly necessary where new designs are contemplated. Too often, however, sketches are omitted when minor changes from regular designs are called for. Rather than depend upon verbal descriptions, even for minor changes, the owner should include sketches as a part of the contract documents.

General Problems in the Award of Contracts. Even the tightest, most competently written specifications will not produce the desired results unless the owner is willing to be fair and consistent in his treatment of bidders. In too many instances care is taken to write good specifications, but the offer of the lowest bidder is accepted even though the bid does not meet specifications. Occasionally, legal action is threatened against an owner who has accepted a bid that fails to meet specifications, but in most cases manufacturers who actually met specifications shrug their shoulders and accept the situation.

On the owner's side, manufacturers are too often unwilling to meet librarians' specifications. In many instances the manufacturer simply bids his standard model XYZ. Librarians and purchasing agents must constantly be on the alert for such practices. To accept a qualified or limiting bid negates every aspect of the most carefully drawn specification and leaves the owner vulnerable to anything the bidder wants to supply.

Acceptance of qualified bids, except for very compelling reasons, is a slap at every conscientious bidder who sincerely tries to meet the specifications. Legally, a qualified bid is cause for automatic rejection, and the owner should not hesitate to take such action when it is indicated. Sometimes every bid may be qualified, in which case it may then be necessary to evaluate all of the products offered. For this reason the General Conditions should contain a clause requiring that any and all deviations from the written specifications be explained in detail in an accompanying letter. Bids qualified in any way without such explanation should be rejected.

Another practice of the alternate or qualified bidder is to propose a different design. To the nontechnical person or committee—and this is a not infrequent occurrence in small and medium-sized public or academic libraries—the alternate proposal looks satisfactory and is accepted. The result, of course, is that the owner has approved the bidder's specifications, which may represent a cheaper quality.

In summary, the following six points should be emphasized:

1. Make certain that the contract documents for library furnishings are as clear, detailed, and complete as possible.

2. Use performance specifications, including laboratory tests wherever possible.

3. If the term "or equal" is used, cite three comparable items instead of one and identify the person or persons who will determine what is "equal."

4. Do not establish criteria for bidders unless such criteria will be followed.

5. Do not establish specifications which are not required.

6. Do not accept qualified bids; legally they may be thrown out without further consideration.

DISCUSSION

Question from the floor: What about the timing of samples for finish tests?

MR. POOLE: In most cases samples should be received prior to the opening of bids. But it makes little difference whether they are received far enough in advance of the bid opening to be tested or not, as long as you have the samples in your possession. They may be tested before or after the opening of bids. Usually it will take a testing laboratory a week to ten days to go through a complete schedule of finish tests. Some tests require twenty-four to forty-eight hours, in a moisture chamber or in a heat oven, depending upon which test is being run.

But if the samples are tested within ten days or two weeks after the opening bids, there is still plenty of time to make the award unless the delivery schedule is tight. Ordinarily, there will be from thirty to sixty days to award bids after they have been opened. The time from bid opening to award is usually stated in the contract documents.

Question from the floor: Your remarks were directed primarily toward furnishings of new buildings. What about the problem of adding equipment to a building in which one wants to match existing equipment? How does one write specifications to get matching equipment?

MR. POOLE: It is not difficult to write specifications to match finishes, although it is more difficult to write specifications to match designs. Nevertheless, as Captain Waters pointed out this morning, you are in control because it is your money. You have a right to specify whatever you believe and can document what is required for your furnishings and for your equipment.

In other words, you have the right to say what you need, provided it is reasonable. I think this is one of those situations in which you can reasonably say that the furniture on a given bid must match in design and in finish some particular item you already own. I do not think any authority would quarrel about the need to provide a harmonious grouping of library furnishings. So write the specifications to require that. Obviously, the original manufacturer can meet those specifications, and it may be that some other manufacturers can, too; if not, the number of bidders may be reduced. But you will still have a viable bid.

Comment from the floor: I did not hear you mention workmen's compensation and contractors' comprehensive liability insurance in cases where men are on the project. These are important to have, particularly for libraries, because many problems arise which require such insurance.

In the case of unit prices, there is the advantage of splitting the contracts; in other words, it may not be desirable to give all the office furniture, for instance, to one vendor. We have found that we can often get just as good equipment in performance and specifications and save 10 or even 15 percent if we split the various items among the various bidders.

In connection with shop drawings, we find it desirable to include illustrations of items we are specifying by catalog number. It is easy to transpose a number and get an item that is not exactly the one wanted.

MR. POOLE: Usually, workmen's liability insurance and workmen's compensation are legal requirements. Certainly they do form an important part of the bid documents.

Comment from the floor: I have a comment on the problem of matching existing equipment. Today many of the larger jobs are funded under the Higher Education Facilities Act, the regulations of which take precedence over the owner's detailed specifications. These regulations contain a very loose "or equal" clause, which states that if the product performs the function essentially as described, it must be considered equal.

Under this clause there is a real question in my mind whether what is needed to match present equipment can be obtained. If nothing else would do the job and the present equipment must be interchanged with the new, it might be well to go out without asking for competitive bids. Although most manufacturers provide similar products, they are not necessarily identical and do not provide the interchangeability that may be desired.

MR. POOLE: We are probably going to be faced in the next few years with many changes in our way of doing things because of federal requirements. The manufacturers probably have the most experience because they are beginning to meet these government requirements. Perhaps this is a place for negotiating a contract, if you are permitted to do so by the law in your jurisdiction.

Question from the floor: Please comment about the desirability of and preparation of alternate specifications. I am thinking particularly of a case in which we are dealing with two bidders who use different materials.

MR. POOLE: In building situations, alternates are very frequently taken, and I see no reason why, if you are involved with two different types of products and are willing to accept either type, you cannot take alternate bids. On the other hand, if you want a particular design for justifiable reasons, you have a right to insist on the one you want. Usually, alternate bids are taken to afford some flexibility in cost.

Comment from the floor: In a situation in which we can get only one manufacturer to supply the basic items we want, and another manufacturer can supply a different item which performs the same function, we write the specifications for both of them, so that we can select either specification if the contract is awarded.

MR. POOLE: If you are willing to accept either one of two types of products, you can put out specifications for both and then award the bid based upon the lowest price.

Comment from the floor: There is one clarification I would like to have. You said that if the finish is good, you frequently accept the other details as being all right, because the finishing is the most expensive part of the process. You assume that if the manufacturer puts on an expensive finish, he probably has done a good job all the way through. However, we have high-density plastic laminates that have excellent finishes, and the basic cost of these is not so great that the manufacturer could not bond a finish of that type to a wood surface and pass it off with questionable details underneath. Would you clarify this point?

MR. POOLE: When I spoke of tests for finishes, I was thinking of finishes on natural wood, either solids or veneers. If you are writing specifications for actual wood finishes, then you can require tests which will distinguish between a good finish and a bad finish.

Any good commercial testing laboratory can run a series of tests which will determine whether the finishes submitted do or do not meet specifications. In most cases the manufacturer who has a quality product in every other respect has a first-rate finish, and vice versa. This is not always true, however, and the quality of the finish should be considered only as a general guide to overall quality. Quality of finish is not a suitable guideline, however, for evaluating products which use plastic laminates. These are in a different category altogether.

Let me comment at this point on another subject. Earlier it was suggested that librarians might use specifications prepared by General Services Administration. I would like to suggest that this be done with caution. The Library Technology Program spent a good deal of time and money in looking into established specifications and found that very few were useful for library purchases. In the past the General Services Administration has not devoted its energies to establishing useful specifications for library furnishings. However, I understand that the Library Technology Program is currently undertaking a project with GSA to establish performance specifications for library technical furniture and perhaps some other types of library furnishings. Hopefully, we will see useful specifications developed by this program.

Comment from the floor: Is it not true that more and more furniture is being made with plastic-laminate surfaces rather than with straight veneers? Veneers have disadvantages, too, and the buyer has to expect scratches, chipping, and similar problems which require repair. Should we not consider that aspect of it?

MR. POOLE: Yes, I think we should, but I do not think we have enough information yet to say that one is better than the other in all circumstances. The Library Technology Program looked into this at some length, but was unable to find a satisfactory answer. Real wood veneers, which are more expensive than plastics, seem to provide the better table surface in the long run. The plastic laminates are perhaps better in the short run. Formica and similar materials are very durable, but when the finish is gone, it is gone. The only thing that can be done is to strip off that sheet of plastic and put on a new one. This is an expensive process. On the other hand, finishes on natural wood veneer may not last as long as the plastics, but they can be refinished at less cost. Many persons believe that natural wood has a depth of finish and a warmth that plastic cannot match. You must make your own decision.

Comment from the floor: Part 16 of the American Society for Testing and Materials Code that came out last week has a section on laminates and woods which I think will help the man with the question on laminates versus veneers.

Comment from the floor: I get the impression here today that librarians are expected to be able to write highly technical specifications in great detail. I just wonder how many people like myself feel totally inadequate to do that.

Furthermore, I wonder if we are putting enough emphasis on the fact that architects and their staffs are available to do not only the planning and engineering of the buildings, but also to plan furniture and furnishings. Then they are responsible for the total effect. It is probably good for us to learn some of this lingo and to seem intelligent about it, but in attempting to write specifications for bonding veneer and other technical requirements, I wonder if we are not getting in a little too deep.

I want to raise another question concerning the public relations side of awarding contracts. When bids are opened in a town conscious of being a town, not a New York, the buyer has a responsibility to local business which he may not like, but which still he has to recognize. Particularly in purchasing furniture and furnishings, he must consider the local vendors. The local taxpayer expects some allowance to be made for dealing with local businessmen. I would be glad to have an objective comment on that.

Finally, in connection with cost, it seems to me that specifying custom furniture and equipment that is made to specifications and requires tests is certainly going to increase the cost of equipment and materials and possibly reduce the number of bidders substantially. This question of cost ought to come in, because if standard items that are being produced—most of which are good quality—can be used, it is much better than trying to stop a factory, stop regular production, and make something that is different.

MR. POOLE: Somewhere in my remarks I stated that the librarian could scarcely be expected to write detailed specifications, or to know the complete makeup of bid documents, or to be able to write the bid documents. However, we have always taken the position that these Institutes should provide librarians with the background to make them at least familiar with the terminology and with some of the situations they are going to face in planning and equipping a new building.

I believe that the price of the building and the furnishings you want is your willingness to devote time to the task. This may not be your job. You are much more involved in the administration of your library and your other problems. You should not be expected to be an architect, a consultant, and everything else rolled into one. Yet it is true in many cases that, to the extent you can be knowledgeable about your requirements for a building and furnishings, that building and those furnishings will neet your needs more effectively.

Many of you have faced, or will in the future face, these problems. Only by being exposed to them, by hearing some of the terminology, and by having access to written information about them can you be knowledgeable about them. Otherwise, you are forced to leave all details to the architect and the purchasing agent. I believe you should be knowledgeable even though you cannot be an expert. All we have intended to do here is to provide useful background.

The matter of public relations is certainly an important one in the award of bids. Qualifications of local suppliers differ with each locality. This is a problem the librarian must solve in his own situation. Certainly he must consider to what extent he is willing to sacrifice quality or particular requirements in order to make it possible for some local vendor to bid. But this is his decision.

It is true that custom-designed furnishings cost more than standard, off-the-shelf items. Almost no manufacturer will break into a regular production line without charging for it. However, if your budget is good, if you have a $5,000,000 building of outstanding design, you are not going to install run-of-the-mill furnishings if they do not harmonize with that building. If you have a $500,000 building, you are probably going to use stock items because that sort of budget does not permit custom design. Again, it is a matter of keeping things in balance. If the architect is designing a very fine building with a very substantial budget, both you and he will want the furnishings that go into that building to complement the design. Sometimes the furnishings do not complement the building. Then the aesthetic effect can be disastrous.

Do what you can with the budget prepared. If you cannot afford custom-designed furniture, then you must pick stock items. If you pick stock items, you have to know how to do it without getting the worst furniture on the market.

Comment from the floor: You mentioned that by going through a local vendor, the buyer might have to sacrifice quality. Any reputable manufacturer that he would want to do business with has local representatives or dealers in many cities. All of us have access to these reputable manufacturers, so

I do not understand your statement that one has to sacrifice quality by going through local vendors.

MR. POOLE: Many of the quality manufacturers do have representatives serving the smaller communities and, thus, available to the librarian, but this is by no means true in all cases, and this is the point. In other words, the librarian may have on his board supplier XYZ who does not handle a line of quality furnishings. Instead, he handles a line that is down near the bottom. Or perhaps someone who gave money for the building represents a manufacturer or has a friend who sells a line that is of poor quality. Or, more frequently, the sole dealer in office furniture in some community sells only the lower-quality lines. The dealer ten miles away may handle the top-quality line, but the librarian has to deal with the man in his home town, not the man in the next town.

The problem is not that the quality lines are unavailable, but that the librarian may be in a position where he feels he has to support someone who handles a poor product. I know of one case in which a prominent board member sells industrial shelving. No librarian wants that kind of shelving. Yet the librarian involved has to see that this man has an opportunity to bid. The only way he can avoid purchasing this industrial shelving is to write performance specifications which eliminate this product. Yet he still has to see that the man gets a chance to bid. This is a public relations matter.

There may be situations in which for some reason a particular firm or individual should have an opportunity to bid. You may want him to get the bid; at the same time, you may not want the product he is furnishing. You have to evaluate the matter in terms of the situation in the local community.

Comment from the floor: As a designer and specifier of interiors, I want to comment about alternate specifications. It was suggested that, with the possible exception of metal or wood shelving, alternate specifications that mix up wood and metal or various kinds of manufacturing designs virtually require writing two sets of specifications in order to offer alternate specifications. While I think it would not cause difficulty in shelving, it is quite a different matter with other furnishings. Are you really willing to pay for two sets of specifications?

Comment from the floor: I am a representative of a manufacturer. The things you have been talking about are the specifications that eventually end up on our desk. We read dozens of them every week. Hardly a week goes by that we do not find a situation which we do not know how to handle.

One problem is that the specifications seldom indicate on what basis the award will be made. Earlier there were comments that the job does not have to go to low bidder. It can be the lowest bidder, the lowest responsible bidder, etc. I suggest that it would be well to put into the specifications that the award will be made to the lowest responsible bidder or to indicate the actual basis upon which the award will be made.

Recently, I reviewed a bid in which unit prices were required. The inference was that all items of a certain class would be let to no more than one manufacturer. On this basis there was apparently a low bidder. It turned out that the bids exceeded the available funds by 50 percent. Then they juggled the unit prices. They deleted this and that, and all at once there was a different low bidder. This has not been resolved yet. But if it had been clearly stated how this award would be made, it might have made a difference in our pricing.

For the manufacturer who has to estimate this kind of job, the situation is like a building. If you have a clean building with the general contractor, it is better. The clearer your specifications concerning the basis of award, the better your opportunities will be for good prices.

I do not think anything is changing faster than specifications or purchasing procedures for library furnishings. The government has had a tremendous influence on this. It might be well to prequalify bidders. Recognizing that Uncle Sam is looking over your shoulder with requirements, you might indicate that bidders are to specify what they propose to furnish. Then you would tell them before the bids were open whether or not these are acceptable. This would be helpful because after the bids are opened, you would not have the arguments that often occur.

Samples are another pet peeve of ours. Not that we mind furnishing samples, but there is nothing more disconcerting than to spend $100 to air freight a sample to meet a severe deadline and then find that all at once the owner realized that everybody did not get their samples there, so he decided to waive the requirement for providing samples.

This is not a joke and it happens more frequently than you would believe. I am embarrassed to think how many manufacturers, including myself, have failed to meet the requirement of providing samples. So the one thing we should be aware of and stick to is not to put anything in specifications that is not really needed. When the decision is made, be impartial and objective, stick to the specifications, and make the awards on that basis. There has to be integrity on both sides for this to work to the advantage of everyone.

MR. POOLE: I agree completely that we have to have integrity on the part of both owner and bidder. When specifications are written, be sure that nothing is put in them that is not required. There have been too many cases in which some part of the specifications has been waived to accommodate a given manufacturer.

Comment from the floor: I am an interior designer. One gentleman mentioned that he would feel uncomfortable to think that he, as a librarian, would be required to have the knowledge to write a specification. The great value in a librarian's having some knowledge of specifications is not the unlikely occurrence that he would actually have to write the specifications, but to help him better understand the specifications. As specifiers, we often have difficulty in getting librarians interested enough in specification writing. Once it gets past the point of establishing the general configuration and the dimensions of the equipment, when we get down to the nuts-and-bolts or performance part of the specifications, we have found too frequently that the librarian's interest in the specification wanes because he lacks knowledge in this area. We would like to see more librarians question or challenge us, to make us perform at our best in providing good specifications.

There was a point brought up about controlling the "or equal" in specifications. I think the prequalification of bidders is an excellent procedure. If it can be arranged, it can help any librarian get what he wants. However, this is sometimes difficult, particularly when working with government agencies which require reasonably open competition. Once the bids are in, it is sometimes difficult to get a very low bid thrown out on the basis of noncompliance with the specifications. If such noncompliance can be established prior to bidding, it is much better than to let the manufacturer or vendor bid the job when he is not in compliance with the specifications.

One thing we try to do is to bring a deeper self-examination of the requirements of libraries by the librarians involved. The same thing applies to specification writing. The details of construction required should be examined to see what really is needed.

Earlier the general specifications governing the quality and design of library furnishings and equipment were discussed. We have found that many of the general woodwork specifications available, such as those developed by GSA, are inadequate when applied to library equipment. However, woodwork construction specifications which we find establish adequate quality for this field are available from the Architectural Woodworkers Institute. The Institute has established three grades of construction, and you can select the standard, custom, or premium grade—whichever you can afford. These specifications are very detailed and even go so far as to establish the size of a gauge to determine whether a joint between two pieces of wood is acceptable. Properly used, these specifications will help obtain first-quality woodwork. In some instances, however, we have used these specifications and still have been unable to obtain the quality necessary for library needs because they were not enforced.

All too frequently, the architect, the librarian himself, or the designer on a job, when a government institution is involved, is stripped of some degree of control in the implementation of specifications. Sometimes the items delivered to the job do not conform to the specifications, or when the item is delivered to the job, it may not be the same thing presented in samples. These items should be spot-checked, too.

Comment from the floor: In discussing specifications there was some talk about qualifications and standards and whether you are willing to accept them. Certainly librarians—and, I would add, most architects—do not know much about the kinds of joints that should be used in furniture. Manufacturers have made a thorough study of these details.

If we want steel desks, we can look at a dozen different steel desks and tell which ones would be acceptable. Then why can we not forget trying to describe how those steel desks are made and do exactly the kind of thing that the government does when it buys a truck, or automobile, or something else? It specifies a one-and-a-half-ton Ford truck or a Chevrolet truck. With regard to bidders and bidder qualifications, which you spoke of in your formal talk, what about having a selected bidder list? As long as five or six of the manufacturers who promise to be fully acceptable are included, why cannot the list just be restricted to them?

MR. POOLE: I know many situations in which you cannot do that by law.

Comment from the floor: If you cannot, then you do something else.

MR. POOLE: You cannot specify just a Ford truck in many state and municipal situations because Chevrolet has a right to bid on that truck also. If manufacturer XYZ has three dovetail joints in his card catalog and you specify three dovetail joints, you will eliminate all of the other manufacturers who may have only two dovetail joints. Ordinarily, you are not justified in specifying one manufacturer over another, and this is why performance specifications are so important.

Comment from the floor: In the example you gave, you are again trying to define the number of joints, and this is what I am saying you should not be doing, because we do not know anything about them.

MR. POOLE: No, I definitely am not trying to specify the number of joints. On the contrary, I am saying we should specify performance rather than details of construction. In selecting steel stacks we ought not be concerned with how many nuts or bolts or what the gauge of steel is. We should be concerned with performance. This means how many pounds per square foot a shelf will take before it deflects too much or how many pounds the total stack will support before the column begins to bend past an acceptable point. I have seen steel stacks with columns that would bend three inches and keep on bending. This is pretty poor performance. In the case of wood furniture, it is much more difficult to specify performance. Yet we have for years, as you point out, tried to establish detailed specifications in terms of the number of joints and so forth. This is the thing that is restrictive. We should get away from that to the extent we can. But we cannot go out and specify brand XYZ unless we do it on a legitimate basis.

Question from the floor: How many states will not allow a restrictive bidder list?

MR. POOLE: I know a number which will not permit a restrictive bidder list, but the manufacturers are in a better position to answer this than I am. Any firm that wants to bid must be allowed to do so. Anybody can walk in off the street and be given a set of bid documents. He may not qualify later, but he is entitled to bid.

Comment from the floor: Bids must be advertised publicly, and an opportunity to bid must be provided to anybody who can put up a bond. In the projects we work on, they are entitled to take out a set of plans and present a bid.

Comment from the floor: We certainly do not have to in Michigan.

Comment from the floor: I would like to comment on the prequalification of bidders. We have recently done this and were successful in public work where the Housing and Home Finance Agency was involved.

Comment from the floor: The example of HHFA, which is now part of Housing and Urban Development, or HUD, does not answer all problems. For example, just before I came, I worked on a library in southern Minnesota where, under HUD, three alternates for each product had to be presented. The question then arises, are the three alternates in fact equal? Let me give you an example of the problems we faced. The architect in this case wanted to buy chair A, but to do this he had to specify two other chairs, so he picked chairs B and C. When the bids came out, chair A was $195, chair B was $205, and chair C was $110.

Now the chair that he wanted to buy happened to be one that I represented. I made my bid on the chair through my dealer. The architect had to buy under HUD, who insisted that he take the lowest of the three presumed to be equal. The architect usually determines what is equal among the three specified, but not always.

MR. POOLE: Specification of three generally comparable lines would often be a solution and a much better procedure than specifying only one, but certainly there are circumstances such as you describe which are different.

Our discussion today has shown that there are many problems and in some instances no good answers for these problems. Every jurisdiction is different. We have heard about the possibility of using a restricted bidder list and about buying by brand name. In some areas, however, these methods may not be permissible, and more traditional procedures have to be used. Where they are permissible, they can certainly be used to the owner's advantage. All you can hope to do is to be familiar with these general problems, in order to talk intelligently with your purchasing agent. Where you know of a device that has worked elsewhere, you can suggest that this be used.

Problems in the Preparation of Specifications for Library Furnishings and Equipment
A Panel Discussion

Moderator:
   FRAZER G. POOLE
   Director, Library
   University of Illinois, Chicago Circle
   Chicago, Illinois

Panel Members:
   CHARLES WARD
   Architect, Library Design Associates
   Tulsa, Oklahoma

   DONALD E. BEAN
   Library Management and
   *   Building Consultants, Inc.*
   Evanston, Illinois

   A. R. ZIMMERMAN
   Furniture and Furnishings Branch
   Standardization Division
   General Services Administration
   Washington, D.C.

   ROBERT H. ROHLF
   Coordinator of Building Planning
   Library of Congress
   Washington, D.C.

MR. WARD:

The problem of using "or equal" in furniture specifications is an extremely difficult one. It certainly is not one that you as librarians should be expected to answer, but you should be aware of the ramifications and, in some cases, the remedies open to you. Our firm does not use the phrase, since we find it to be a meaningless expression. Let me say, however, that you cannot discard it lightly. You must have competent legal counsel to advise you when and how you can do it, as well as of the other legal avenues open to you to achieve what you want in the furniture for your library.

It occurred to me that a number of the questions raised this afternoon need not be problems if you approach your building program in good order. I fear some of you may feel that writing specifications for furniture is done in white heat two weeks before you intend to occupy the library. I am sure it has been done precisely that way. Speaking as an architect, I

think selection of the interior furnishings for your library is as critical to the success of that library, both functionally and aesthetically, as the design of the building. In too few cases is proper consideration given to the selection of furniture. After all, the specifications are only an expression of decisions that have been made previously.

Libraries are unique architectural problems. Your objective and your mission should be to bring a patron and a book together as efficiently, conveniently, and in as pleasant an atmosphere—an atmosphere conducive and inviting to study and reading—as possible. Every building type is unique, but the design of a library poses a problem different from any other that an architect faces.

To plan and design your building, you need four very important people, each of whom must contribute in a specialized way to the whole program if you are going to have a totally successful library. In our practice we believe in the concept of total design. This appears new to some people, but it is the only intelligent way to approach a building problem: the design of the building, the furniture, the grounds, the site—everything that goes into the library.

The first person you need is the librarian, and the success of your library is to a great extent dependent upon the knowledge, the enthusiasm, and the background that he brings to the building team. One of the most important decisions you will be called upon to make during the entire life of the building is the selection of the architect. Rarely do you get a better building than the best building that the architect has previously done. In other words, you should see the work of the architect; you should see what he considers to be his best work and decide if he is capable of the architecture you want. This man should be sympathetic to the problem in hand and should be competent in the field of interior design. That is a large order, but there are architects who fill that order. The third person is the chairman of the building committee—a member of the board of trustees, the university architect, or a member of the faculty. The fourth, and an extraordinarily valuable and important member of the team, is the consultant. The success of the library depends on this team.

These four people are responsible for writing the building program. Earlier, Mr. Poole, Mr. Bean, and I were discussing the writing of the program, and I found each of us had different notions as to what should be in that program. I would wager that in this assembly we could find as many approaches to writing a program as there are people sitting here. In my opinion, the program should deal not only with what a library should be, but should suggest an intelligent approach to achieving that library. It covers site considerations, design criteria, architectural considerations, internal arrangements, departmental analysis, environmental considerations, furnishings, and artistic enrichment. It should contain the librarian's statement, a discussion of the budget, and probably miscellaneous bibliographical material.

The selection of furniture begins with the writing of the program. Make some determination even at that early date on the general character of the furnishings which you feel are appropriate to your library. This is not to say that the program, when completed, is something graven on stone, immovable and unchangeable, but it certainly should be a guide to lead you through the building process.

A sound program is the best insurance that the librarian, architect, consultant, and chairman of the building committee can have. I cannot overemphasize this. It will be a document useful long after the building is completed. From this the architect prepares a schematic drawing which shows graphically what has already been expressed verbally in the program. It shows the areas, their interrelationship, etc. The schematic drawing may go through many revisions. It is important that the furniture be outlined in that schematic in general areas. Locations of bookstacks, tables, carrels, lounge furniture, charging desk, and other equipment should be shown.

From schematic drawings are developed a set of drawings which are usually called preliminaries. These spell out in great detail where the partitions are. It refines areas and rooms and indicates in detail the reading areas, the arrangement of the stacks, the relationship of stacks to lounge furniture, etc. This is the design development phase, which simply means that you have now finalized your thinking. You may change it, but you know at this stage, before the working plans are drawn and specifications for the building are written, the general type of furniture you want. From these schematics and preliminary drawings the architect can intelligently develop the working drawings for the building.

You can purchase furnishings in three different categories. Much of the furniture can probably be built economically as part of the general contract. If that is your decision, it should go in the working drawings. In many cases peripheral shelving and such items as the charging desk and filing cabinets may be part of the general contract and probably can be purchased much more economically in that way.

There is a second group of loose, or movable, furniture such as bookstacks, lounge furniture, table and chairs, seating units, display cases, and similar items. You should decide at this time whether this furniture is going to be standard off-the-shelf equipment or whether it is going to be specially designed. The statement was made earlier that custom-built furniture is more expensive. This is not necessarily so. As a matter of fact, intelligently designed custom furniture can actually be more economical.

You have three areas of choice to make, but I want to emphasize again that you should begin as far in advance of the construction of the building as possible to compile the plans and specifications which will become the contract documents for the purchase of your furniture. To do this, you should avail yourself of the opportunity to see a number of libraries in action; you should go to places like the Merchandise Mart in Chicago or to some other place with a comprehensive display of furniture. Do not limit yourself to the furniture that is in the usual library line. There is excellent furniture in many commercial fields which you can profitably and economically use. The architect and the consultant should be aware of this possibility, too, and your judgment should be made on the best piece of furniture for your library.

When this judgment is made and crystallized, you are ready to write the specifications. As has been observed previously, this is an extraordinarily difficult document to prepare. You must set up a bidding document which is fair to the people you are asking to bid and which at the same time will give you the furniture you want.

Much of the discussion this afternoon was about nuts-and-bolts specifications and performance specifications. In my view it is almost impossible to write either a performance specification or a nuts-and-bolts specification for a chair. If you want an Eames chair, or a Knoll chair, or a Jens Risom chair for your library, that is precisely what you should specify. You should be aware of the other chairs available to you, but if one of these named fits your need aesthetically and is what you need in the library, then that is what you should have.

Now I come to the problem of the phrase "or equal." In my view there is no such thing as an "equal to" piece of furniture. I am speaking now of a chair or possibly a sofa. If you say that you want Knoll chair XYZ, then there is no other chair on the market like it. When you say "or equal," you are saying something that is meaningless; there cannot possibly be an equal to it.

I suggest this alternative. If there are two chairs that you will accept, list those two chairs. Certainly is is ridiculous to specify a chair that costs $45 and also one that costs $35 and expect to get a competitive bid. There are comparable units in various manufacturers' lines which you can intelligently specify, each of which may be acceptable to you.

A very, very important criterion is the looks or design of the furniture you are placing in your building. Do not come out with a Queen Anne building and Marie Antoinette furniture. Make the furniture homogeneous, complementary, and, hopefully, a lovely part of the building. If you began thinking about furniture the day that you and the architect first met to talk about your building, you will come up with the furniture that you want—furniture that is compatible with the building, and furniture at a competitive price.

MR. BEAN:

Many of the statements already made at this meeting appear controversial, but I think they are due rather to different perspectives. In a sense, the things that we have discussed constitute the form and not the substance of what we are after. What are we after? What is the goal of this purchasing procedure? I like to think of it as obtaining the most suitable furniture for the library, considering all elements, of which cost or price is one. The key words are "most suitable" because in some cases furniture of good quality should be purchased; in other cases furniture of low quality is perfectly satisfactory. We do need perspective.

I would like to leave two main thoughts with you. First, no specification, however carefully written, should be depended upon as the only, or even the major, means of securing the desired type and quality of equipment. It is surprising how many people do not realize this but rather assume that the specifications will protect their interests. As the old song goes, "It ain't necessarily so." Second, the successful purchase of suitable equipment requires time and effort on the part of those who make decisions.

I said that no specification, however carefully written, should be depended upon as the only or major means of securing the type and quality of equipment that is desired. I learned that lesson very early in my former career in the equipment business. In the 1930's, during the days of the federal Public Works Administration, the University of Arkansas erected a library building. There was reason for me to believe that we wanted high-quality equipment. The architect was a capable man who had to follow federal regulations regarding purchasing. For five days he and I sat at a table thinking out and writing specifications for that equipment. Every conceivable detail of manufacture was covered. They started with the quality of wood: the nature, the drying of the wood—first in the open air, six months for every half-inch thickness of stock—and then the drying process for moisture content. There were twenty-four different kinds of planing and drying operations called for, besides a host of other details.

Then what happened? Samples were furnished as called for, and the low bidder, which was a large, reputable, and responsible firm, was awarded a contract. Some years later the table tops sagged. The manufacturer claimed the specifications should have called for a center pedestal, which was unique because if those table tops had been made with the proper quality and care they would not have sagged, and center pedestals, as you know, are a handicap if they are not needed. Probably the trouble was that no matter how expert one is in judging furniture, the very factors which are most important in governing the quality of the equipment—particularly wood equipment—are intangible and cannot be seen or tested except at certain points. Even if they could be tested, what opportunity does a small library have to make tests, and what assurance can there be that the wood actually furnished is comparable to the carefully made sample which was tested?

What then can be put into the specifications that will be of practical assistance? Among those items are two which are not used often enough. One requires each bidder to indicate the source of his manufacture for each item. For some items, do not be content with merely listing the item. For instance, in the case of catalogs, it is required that the name of the manufacturer be given of the catalog trays, the catalog shelves, and the catalog bases. For tables the name of the manufacturer of the table tops is required separately from the manufacturer of the table bases. Why is this? Because I have known many cases in which the manufacturers of parts of items were different, and this was quite important to know. In many cases a firm purchased table tops, put the legs on them, and called themselves table manufacturers. Also included in the specifications should be a stipulation that the contractor, before being paid, shall be required to furnish a notarized affidavit signed by an officer of the company stating that the equipment was in fact manufactured by the factories stated in the bid of the contractor.

You are faced with two possible dangers. The company may lack integrity, so that if it gets into a financial pinch, some item of inferior quality may be substituted. Or the manufacturer may have very high standards, but the man in charge of negotiating the contract may indulge in some questionable practices. I am not saying that equipment people are dishonest, but there are a few chiselers in this business, as there are in every business, and they make it tough for the customers in many more cases than is realized. In such instances you may have some equipment made by cheaper suppliers not mentioned in the bid.

I have known of several instances in which equipment is bid and ostensibly made by library equipment manufacturers which could not have been made by any of them. Yet the customer cannot determine this until after several seasonal changes, from winter to summer and summer to winter. In this connection we must realize that the more complicated the technical specification, the greater the danger that you are playing into the hands of the very people against whom you may wish to protect yourselves. You are playing their ball game on their home grounds. The experienced manager of an equipment contract knows how to cut corners better than you know how to detect them.

I have been involved in hundreds of biddings in almost every state, and I have taken many contracts on a mere informal exchange of letters. So far as I know, every customer received his last nickel's worth in agreements to which I have given my word, particularly when it was a matter of faith. I think that this response to trust is the human thing to do, but in the very nature of preparing specifications you set yourself up as an antagonist to the supplier who has absolutely no obligation to you beyond what is written in those specifications. Now, you may have lost that important relationship as a valued or preferred customer or client. You have become a party to a contract, and you may not be entitled to one bit more than is written into that contract. My entreaty is: beware. In these circumstances what more can be done to protect yourselves? Anything you can do may be inadequate, but here are a few procedures that have helped in the past.

1. Require in the specifications that the bidder list a certain number of installations he has made which are at least five years old. I prefer to take those which are at least five years old because then they have been through some seasonal changes. Ask for installations within a certain radius from your library of a magnitude approximately equal to your contemplated purchase.

2. Require the statement in the specifications that the manufacturers of the equipment listed in the bid are the same as those that furnished the equipment in the installation referred to in all items. In other words, a company may list a library as an installation, but it may have furnished only a very small part. The bidder should be required to list what he actually did furnish.

3. Here is a point so important that all previous care will go for naught if it does not follow. You must visit the installations listed by any bidder whom you are seriously considering, and this takes a lot of time. You must examine those installations meticulously in connection with your own past experience, and you must talk with the people there about maintenance problems. This is the part of the purchasing procedure that is most likely to fall down. Public library trustees are busy and their jobs are sometimes rather thankless. Purchasing departments are hard pressed to find the time to make these vital investigations. Too much dependence is placed on specifications of the manufacturer with the hope that all will be well in the end. Do not allow this to happen. Insist that your board or your purchasing authority make this investigation with you or rely on your judgment in the selection of the contractors.

What else can be done to protect yourselves in this bidding process? Investigate the person who will execute your contract. This is usually the salesman involved. Talk with some of his other customers. Establish as well as you can an estimate of his ability and his integrity. Both are important to the success of your project.

Some of you have had extensive experience in the equipping of library buildings. The library equipment company may not have a person of your experience. If the company has the necessary integrity, that company will not object to the safeguards which you build into your specifications. The main criterion is the experience on the part of the individual or company whom you engage.

There is a little item of the philosophy of Whittier relevant to our discussion: "In many instances the goal has become obscured." The goal of obtaining the most suitable furniture has become obscured because of the buyers' overdependence on certain purchasing procedures and methods. Too often these procedures have been relied upon as a substitute for expert judgment and as a substitute for investigations necessary to obtain the basis for that judgment.

The library may suffer, however, if librarians, architects, board members, college administrators—any of those who constitute the buying team—rely on the procedures, and little else, to bring about the purchase which best suits the library's interests. The difficulty is compounded by the notion that the low bidder must be the successful bidder, unless it can be proven that his work is not acceptable. This puts the burden of proof on the wrong party. This philosophy of purchasing may be an easy way for the purchaser to feel relieved of responsibility. Too often the future operation of the library suffers from the inadequacy of the equipment and the expense of its maintenance. A good purchasing attitude involves the willingness to accept the responsibility of making a judgment based upon evidence which sometimes is difficult to secure, and the courage to stand by that judgment.

There is another philosophy of purchasing which may be called the "grab bag" philosophy. Specifications are written which are fair to all prospective bidders, and the lucky low bidder pulls out the prize. Sometimes this method is carried to such extremes that one might think that the purpose of the bidding is to bring business opportunity to the bidders, instead of to procure the most suitable equipment for the library. Under the rules of this game, any detail of manufacture—no matter how advantageous to the library—which is exclusive to one bidder is eliminated from the specifications. The standards of the specifications tend to be lowered so that all who are regularly in the business can bid. There is nothing wrong with that idea. The danger comes in combining such an approach with the belief that one of the low bidders should be chosen as the supplier, when it is quite possible that the highest bidder's offer in the best for the particular library's interest. In such cases judgment and courage on the part of the purchaser are needed.

What do the terms "lowest bidder" and "best bidder" mean? What is the "lowest and best bid"? What does the word *best* mean? What does the term "lowest responsible bidder," which now appears in federal specifications, mean? Does it mean financial responsibility? Does it mean a reputation for carrying out specifications of the nature of yours? In answering these questions judgment is important and the courage to stand by your judgment is vital.

MR. ZIMMERMAN:

Quality is not written into specifications; quality inspection, quality control, is. The problem in our division is that librarians are not capable of making an effective determination of what is "equal" or "not equal." Our people who buy are not equal. Our people buy fire trucks, and pliers, and automobiles. Our procurement people are probably the worst people at buying library furniture who ever lived; they do not know what they are doing. They do not know furniture per se unless they make a study of it; and unless they know what they are buying, they should not be buying.

We have people in government who read specifications. They read Part 1, which is the open classification of our specification, and they read Part 2, the specifications that are always alleged to be used for fabrics. The construction features are spelled out. If we want a double dowel, we say double dowel. If we want a certain type of glue, we say it should be a certain type of glue. If we want it three-and-a-half inches by three-quarter inch, we say it; we do not beat around the bush about what we want in government furniture.

Section 4 is inspection. If I make a desk with 144 pieces in which one can find fault, any person can reject the desk. Why is not that same opportunity available for library furniture buyers? Why must they be at the mercy of the manufacturer and say, "The manufacturer made this for me, and I don't know whether he did it well or he did it badly." Recall the story about the astronauts going up. They looked at each other and said, "Thank goodness, there are three thousand parts in this thing and they are all made by the lowest bidders. You know, it makes you feel good."

Some day we are going to have equipment that is not made by the lowest bidders; we are going to have equipment made by classified bidders. This is the direction in which federal supply is moving.

Somebody from Remington Rand, or Estey, or Hamilton draws up a specification and it looks good, but you do not know the difference between a good specification and a bad specification. Whom do you take it to? A metallurgist to see whether the metal is good. The woodman to see if the wood is well put together. The statement was made: If it looks good, it is good. That is the biggest thing we fight in government; we know that things that look good are not necessarily good. We know that cheaters can make an item look good. A good furniture manufacturer does not know how to make bad furniture, and a bad manufacturer will never make good furniture. They make furniture—whether it be library or ordinary furniture—equal to their craftsmen's abilities.

We have sent USIA [United States Information Agency] library furniture all around the world. Once, to get one drawer open in a 60-drawer card catalog, we had to pry it apart. The card catalog looked good when it left the United States. It was pretty and it met the specifications, but nowhere in the specifications did it say that the drawers must open and shut. It just said "sixty drawers." We had no recourse with the supplier whatsoever. He said the drawers were there. In that case we wound up with only seventeen drawers that worked after they were pried loose and put back together.

How many of you have ever been in a furniture plant? In how many have you seen pieces of wood put together? How many of you have ever seen steel objects assembled? Some of you drive Chevies, some of you drive Volkswagens, and some of you drive Plymouths. The Cadillac, the Chevrolet, the Plymouth, the Volkswagen—all are made of the same material. What goes into a piece of furniture goes beyond what is in the specification or what the picture looks like. It is the judgment of a craftsman who says that a joint does not quite fit and that he will make it fit or he will take a dimension out and make a new one. That judgment is a necessary element in making furniture.

You can put everything you want into the specifications and everything you want into the inspection, but you still get right back to the integrity of the manufacturer. I know that in the library field today we are spending $25,000,000 to $40,000,000 on shelving alone, and projected figures for the next three years are perhaps $75,000,000 to $100,000,000.

We are charged with writing equipment specifications. I am in charge of purchasing all office furniture in the United States government and all other items made of wood. We have problems: We have walnut shortages; we have "walking" woods, woods that move around. We have bad specifications. We have many reasons why this situation is unpleasant.

I just finished the White House assignment where we did all the furniture. We just finished the Claims and Customs and Patent Appeals courts in Washington. Why does everybody want Jens Risom, and Knoll, and Herman Miller? Why can they not just take good solid furniture? I have nothing against the furniture of these designers. It is excellent.

We are charged with making government specifications, so I met with the Federal Library Committee, which is made up of a representative of every department—Labor, Commerce, Interior, etc. We talked to them about what kind of libraries they wanted, what kind of furniture they wanted. Interior wanted traditional; if it is not fancy, they did not want it. The Federal Aviation Agency happened to be there as an invited guest. If the style was not "way out," they were not happy. NASA wanted it the same way. We tried to determine what kind of furniture they all wanted. We asked five of them, and we got five different answers.

We were in a situation in which if we were to have government specifications on furniture, I would have needed four traditional styles in Georgian—including Queen Anne, Tom and the younger Chippendale, and maybe some Hepplewhite, maybe a little Adam—and would also have to go into Pahlman and other contemporaries. In addition, we have two or three wood finishes. Whatever I come up with becomes standard for United States government libraries.

We have figured out that we only need 1373 pieces of furniture—1373 pieces of furniture in four finishes and three stocks. Now, that is what you are faced with. What do you buy? What do you put into your library? Where do you get started, and how do you proceed?

We are now working on our Part 3, which is construction, and we are going to attempt to set up there and certainly in Part 4, which is our inspection and classification of defects, a very strong method of emphasizing workmanship, which is the important thing. We hope that in this way the federal government will be able to help you.

MR. ROHLF:

Please remember that my remarks are the result of my experiences in public and academic libraries, not of those in planning the new Library of Congress building.

We must keep in mind that we are prepared to fight a good fight so that the local buyer, local library board, college board, or other local authority has the right to set the level of quality which it desires. It should not have to argue this point with anyone. This high standard of quality can be supported either under a bonding authority which the voters have passed or the city

council may have approved, or with the consent of the board of trustees or academic library authority. Under this authority the right to establish the level of quality exists. It may be a low level, a high level, or a medium level; but whatever the level, we have a right to make the decision. We may make the wrong one, but it is our decision.

I think the term "or equal" is virtually meaningless. I have found that when we are involved in spending large amounts of money for furniture, it is best to qualify bidders beforehand. I agree with the statement made earlier that it is easier to discuss a bidder's qualifications before you know his price; it is more difficult to discuss his qualifications after he has become the low bidder. When local regulations do not prohibit it, qualifying bidders beforehand will assure you that when the bids are opened, you will not be faced with the question of whether the low bidder is qualified. Remember when you are buying items in quantity, such as twenty thousand catalog cards, that it is not an imposition to ask for samples beforehand, with a clause inserted that the successful bidder's sample will become the temporary property of the library against which all delivered items will be measured. When you are through with the sample, return it. In many cases this stipulation will scare off the "fringe bidder" because he does not want that handmade sample to be compared with the other items which he might supply later. He knows these other items are not going to measure up against this particular sample, because if they did he could not afford to bid the price he is bidding.

I remember a situation in which approximately one thousand meeting room chairs were specified by various manufacturers' names and catalog numbers, but with this dubious "or equal" clause. The low bidder bid the chair at a price lower than it could be purchased by the distributor of its manufacturer. After some thirty days the low bidder went to the purchasing agent and said, "I made a mistake. I would like to supply those chairs, but I know I really can't afford to do so. I made a mistake on my bid. However, I can supply this other chair for this bid price." The bidder was told, "We don't want the other chair, but we will give you back your bid bond." The purchasing agent should have cashed the bid bond or told the dealer to supply the chair. This particular seller uses the same trick all the time, and he succeeds three fourths of the time. It is why he is always low, because most of the time he does not intend to supply what was specified but something cheaper.

This story shows why you need a bid bond and why you should hold bidders to their bids. If they want to play this game, do not do business with them. When you have a bid performance bond, stick to it and do not give anyone an opportunity to cheat on you.

In another case a purchasing agent told the library board members that they could not buy a particular file which they specified because only one manufacturer made it. The library board replied, "Yes, but you are the purchasing agent who is to buy this item. We are the ones who are supposed to specify what we want." He said, "Oh, no, you are not. My job is to buy the cheapest item I can at the best price for the city, and this file is too expensive. There is only one person who makes it. You are not going to get competitive bids, so I am not going to advertise it for bid." This attitude is something you might run up against. I know that by law in the city where it happened, the purchasing agent cannot do what he said. He is simply the agent of the board, not the specifier.

In another situation, in a city where there was some uncertainty about the amount of money available for furniture, the lounge furniture was purchased in two parts, with the idea that in another year or two the remainder could be bought. The specifications were written and the first bidding went well. When the furniture was finally purchased several months later, there was enough money left to finish the job, and bids were asked on the rest of the lounge furniture. But the second time around, someone came in with a copy of the first items at a much lower price, because copies are always cheaper. The board in question agreed that the copy looked exactly like the other chairs, so it decided to buy the copy. The original manufacturer was justifiably upset because this was not his chair any longer, but someone's copy of his chair and someone's copy of his sofa. Nevertheless, the board said they looked the same. You can go back to the same library, some five or six years later, walk through the lounge area, stand five or ten feet away from the sofa or chairs, and you can see the originals because the copies just did not hold up. They were cheaper because they were built cheaper.

I have a pet peeve against copies. Either you decide what you want, buy ahead of time, and stick with it, or you look back and realize that you do not know what you are buying. It is quite embarrassing to admit you really do not know what you are buying. Copies are not originals; they are not "or equals." They are simply copies.

Another hint I can give to a board equipping a building for the first time is to remember that the burden of proof should be on the seller, not on the buyer. I do not see why the buyer is supposed to prove that something is or is not as good as something else. I think the seller has to prove to the buyer that one item is as good as the other. The tables have turned because buyers have been hesitant. Sellers know all the angles and buyers do not, but the proof should be on the seller and not on the buyer.

There was another case in which there was a dispute over some seating in a particular job, and we ended up with the highest of five bids. A sample of each chair was supplied stripped down piece by piece. When the chairs were stripped down and laid open, the board was able to see the obvious differences between what was specified and what was supplied by the four lower bidders. After seeing the proof it bought the highest-priced chair, and in this case the difference was about $18,000 for approximately five hundred chairs.

You must remember that equipping a library is different from normal day-to-day purchasing operations. This is not Number 2 fuel oil we are buying. (I always refer to it as Number 2 fuel oil because it is so easy to write specifications for Number 2 fuel oil and easy to know all the suppliers of Number 2 fuel oil.) When you want a Miller chair, that is the chair you want, and someone else's chair is not the same. If you specify a Jens Risom table, that is the table you want, and someone else's table is not the same. If you are buying Remington Rand shelving, someone else's shelving is not absolutely identical to that shelving. So you have to know what is the same and what is not the same.

Remember, too, that we are dealing with extremely subjective questions when we talk about furnishing libraries. We have the very crucial question of design. I like to use the term "family of design." The task is to design a library and what goes into it so that everything fits, and so that no one particular object stands out, but that everything is subordinate to the overall effect. Design is extremely tough to argue in specifications unless you really know what you are talking about. One of the problems is that you cannot patent or copyright design. Design is something everybody borrows or copies from everybody else. Herman Miller, with the bucket seat or chair, is the first one to talk about all the copies that have resulted from an excellently designed chair.

A contract is only as good as the faith of the people who sign it, as any attorney will tell you. I do not care what that specification or what that contract says. You are concerned with the good faith of the people on both sides, and I do mean on both sides. There is a lot of "tender-loving care" that goes into the manufacturing of some things, and there is a lot of slapdash construction also. You have to know the inferiors, and you have to know which ones get the "TLC." Both of them have their place.

Also remember that there is some furniture that has a very visual effect. When I look at the audience here, I cannot find any two suits or dresses which are the same, or any accessories worn by more than one person, or even eyeglass frames that are the same, and this is the way furniture is today. It is all a little different, and I think you have the right to pick the pieces you want and let somebody else prove that there is a problem in supplying them. Make sure that the burden lies not on you but on the person who wants to supply you with furniture. I would say that when you are buying you should be positive, because purchasing should be an extremely exciting, challenging, and enjoyable task. I would like to emphasize that you have the right to decide what you want and nobody has the right to take this privilege away from you.

DISCUSSION

THE MODERATOR: Here is a question for Mr. Ward: How can one get away from using the term "or equal"? I think you said that it takes a good lawyer.

MR. WARD: The gist of my remarks was that we should be aware that the document we are talking about preparing entails expenditure of thousands of dollars and in many cases hundreds of thousands of dollars. None of us, neither professional specification writers nor others, should attempt to compile a document involving that amount of public funds without the expert advice of a lawyer versed in the purchasing laws. Your counsel should be experienced in this particular phase because he can suggest methods which will allow you—even though the normal interpretation of the law might say differently—to do what you want to do. What we are trying to do in writing specifications is to expend our funds to the best interest of the whole population. Generally speaking, our laws are drawn to allow you to do that. My point was not that you need a good lawyer per se, but that you are going into a legal area and should proceed with counsel to answer your specific questions.

In every case we specify the chair and the fabric we want and also the steel desk in the finish we want. We set up the bid form in such fashion that an alternate can be submitted, but outline clearly the conditions under which an alternate will be considered. Finally, we define whose obligation it is to make that decision so that there will be no questions in the minds of the suppliers.

You should make the decision on what is best for your library long before you ever get to this stage. I believe the ultimate criterion is that the furniture be compatible with the architecture of the building. This is absolutely mandatory. You cannot have a successful library design without it. As a consequence, you have to specify by individual items what you want in your library. What we do is to call for the item we want. We allow alternates to be bid with the knowledge of who will make the final judgment and on what basis an alternate will be considered. We do not give anyone the option of supplying an alternate on the basis of the bid form.

THE MODERATOR: Although you may have some occasions to use the "or equal" clause, you can modify it so that, in effect, you specify the items you want. Such a modification requires that you sometimes specify two or more items of the same general quality. Whoever prepares the specifications must know the furniture lines available and that they are equal.

Here is a question for Mr. Rohlf: How does one prequalify the bidders?

MR. ROHLF: It can be done in several ways. The method I have used is to decide in advance the design and quality of furniture required and the manufacturers known to be able to produce such furniture. Their names are then listed in the specifications as being eligible to bid on the particular furniture involved. On the other hand, if you use "approved equal" instead of "or equal" then you should say that only bids from bidders who have been approved by the owner will be opened. Others who wish to submit bids should apply to the architect, or whoever is handling the bidding, prior to bid opening for approval.

This must be done so many days beforehand. An addendum is then issued to all bidders who are approved as equal, advising them that certain other bidders were approved. They all know then that something else may be bid, and they know against whom they are bidding. This is the device I have used, and it has worked in cities where purchasing agents have said previously that they had to have the "or equal" clause. This has been a task of education, but in several instances they have agreed to the term "or approved equal."

THE MODERATOR: Again we have an example in which one jurisdiction allows something that another jurisdiction does not. In some areas "approved equal" is forbidden.

MR. ZIMMERMAN: In our library and executive office furniture we are trying to classify manufacturers the way the Department of Defense does those of uniforms. The man who makes overalls does not make uniforms; he is not allowed to bid on them. There is a question of tailoring involved in manufacturing a dress uniform. We are trying to classify our manufacturers and suppliers of government furniture in the executive, subexecutive, and general office categories so that cut-rate outfits are not allowed to bid.

The question of government specifications in library furniture came about because the General Accounting Office keeps track of the money. As you know, our problem in government is money. The USIA was accused of spending too much money because it was using proprietary items. Proprietary items in USIA mean Remington Rand. The Agency was told that it should not have the right to be able to say Remington Rand or equal and be able to prove that there was none equal, so a couple of bids came in where somebody else was considered equal.

Attorneys do not decide what is equal. On paper it can say equal, but as Mr. Rohlf pointed out, after five years a substitute or copy hardly stood under its own weight, and that had probably been considered "or equal." That is a term we shy away from in government.

THE MODERATOR: Why is the government, represented by the General Services Administration, not developing performance standards?

MR. ZIMMERMAN: There is control in regard to the area into which the merchandise is being shipped. There is recognition, though, that there is no such thing as a piece of wood not moving. A 17 inch by 34 inch—especially today with some of our "walking" woods—may be a different dimension tomorrow morning. The wood used in drawer sides, drawer backs, and drawer fronts can all move around, and that is why we are going to metal in drawers. We do not know to what extent it is better. Wood has a certain beauty and a certain individual appearance that cannot be duplicated by metal, but metal units certainly have many advantages.

We ship to the twenty-six or more NATO [North Atlantic Treaty Organization] countries all over the world, including to South Asia. A lot of equipment is going over there, and we are not sure it is going to get there in as good a shape as it was when it left here. A chair may swell up and look like a sofa. If the receiver accepts it as a sofa, we do not complain. Other situations are harder to control; for example, it is hard to get dockside inspection. Inspectors do not have much time to look at equipment and often cannot get it off the boat.

MR. ROHLF: On the question of including furniture in the general contract, was Mr. Ward referring to the building contract?

MR. WARD: Yes.

MR. ROHLF: In my experience there are both disadvantages and advantages in doing that. One of the disadvantages is that the general contractor puts the building together by using subcontractors, and in some cases really does not do anything himself. He subcontracts the job; whatever the subs charge him, he adds to the bill. In some cases it may be 10 percent, 12 percent, or only 9-3/4. When furniture or other equipment is included in a general contract, the contractor puts his override in on that. If you have an architect or someone else capable of assuming the responsibility of the furniture and equipment for you, then it can be handled without the contractor's override. In many cases this is a very real cost problem.

MR. WARD: Your remarks are very well put, Mr. Rohlf. I might reinforce my original statement. Obviously, the contractor wants to make a profit on the work that he puts in. Each case is individual. Much of the furniture in the library we have referred to here is built-in, and judgment has to be made by the architect whether it can be built by the general contractor more economically than it can be installed in units by a furniture supplier. Each case must be analyzed individually, but we came to the conclusion in one instance that much of the furniture—peripheral shelving, charging desk, and many built-in filing cabinets—contributed to and enhanced the usefulness of the building.

As an additional point of information, we let the furniture on that library under four different contracts. This is another avenue open to you to get furniture or a portion of it installed. The same observation may be made in regard to the carpeting. I think specifications are often written so that the carpet is in the general contract. Practice varies in different areas of the country, and in some areas where I have worked, seven or eight different contracts were let on a building. The carpet, for example, is an integral part of the building, as are the other floor coverings. We try to analyze where the best interest of the client lies in each instance and go from there.

Question from the floor: One of you gentlemen remarked that it required five years' experience to qualify for a contract. It seems to me that some reputable suppliers would be precluded thereby from qualifying and perhaps eliminated. This does not seem entirely justifiable. Does this mean that no new business can develop?

MR. BEAN: When you eliminate a bidder because he cannot furnish installations which are five years old, you are not eliminating him, he is eliminating himself. There is plenty of opportunity for a bidder to get his experience in supplying $1000, $2000, $3000, and $4000 orders in libraries which are willing to take a chance. Equipping a new building is a serious matter, and the people who provide the furnishings for that building should be required to prove by their previous installations that they are qualified to do the job. This is why I am in favor of requiring that their installations be five years old. It is not done with the idea of eliminating any bidders. In the library revolution which we are going through, there is enough business for almost everybody in the equipment business.

Question from the floor: How should we interpret the phrase "informalities may be waived by the owner"? I have heard many versions and interpretations of this phrase. For instance, an item may be specified with 1.4 mills thickness, but the owner decides to waive this as an informality and accept 1.05 mills. Or the specifications may call for a sample, but one supplier did not get his sample in on time, and then the owner decides to waive the sample as an informality. These interpretations seem to be stretching things a little bit, and I would just like to know your version of that phrase. It occurs in many specifications.

MR. ROHLF: The phrase is usually not requested by librarians, or library boards, or necessarily specifiers. Often a city or county attorney inserts it in the bid documents as a device by which the buyer protects himself from the machinations of the seller. It gives the buyer the legal right to make any exceptions which in his judgment he should make. He can be sued, but this phrase is presumed to give him legal protection.

I doubt that it does, and have talked to some city attorneys who also doubt it, but nobody pushes the point, and it is one of the things that perpetuate themselves. People use it without being sure what it means, but we do know that it gives you the right to say, for example, "Company A didn't submit its sample, but we will take its bid anyway." Personally, I do not agree with this philosophy. I think it is too bad if Company A did not submit its sample, but its name should be stricken out if the sample did not get in on time. Most city and county attorneys will argue this with you.

Comment from the floor: There seems to be one aspect that is overlooked in discussing furniture and building; that is, whether the bookstacks should be part of the general contract. This is a very serious problem and can be an extremely expensive one.

MR. ROHLF: I have seen it done both ways and have argued both ways. In most cases it is the architect who makes the final decision about how it is to be done. If the bookstacks or stack complex, as opposed to standard shelving, is an integral part of the building or structure, the architect alone can put it through on the general contract. This method gives him one less person to follow around to see that it is done right, and that is probably the overwhelming reason for architects' using this procedure. It means that the general contractor, not the architect, has to supervise the installation of the stacks. Most architects have no experience in supervising the installation of bookstacks, simply because they are afraid of it.

MR. WARD: I would hate to give a blanket answer to that question. The architect must make the judgment. Hopefully, we have arrived at the place where the responsibility of the bidder is an integral part of the bidding process. We are not particularly worried about chasing after a different group of suppliers unless it is in the best interest of the client to do so. In fact, we suggest that our clients let out many contracts when it seems to us to be in their best interests to do so. If the stacks become an integral part of the structure, there would be no question that they should be bid in the general contract.

MR. ROHLF: There is one further point I would like to make. There is a problem in specifying built-in stacks because of a wiring problem that is different from standard shelving. Another reason for including them in the general contract is the difficult problem of coordination. If you have ever listened to two subcontractors argue over the timing of this, you know how troublesome this matter of coordination can be.

Testing and Value Analysis, Part I

Presiding: *FRAZER G. POOLE*
Director, Library
University of Illinois, Chicago Circle
Chicago, Illinois

MISS LIANNE REIMERS
Assistant to the President
Buyers Laboratory, Inc.
New York, New York

PETER JACOBS
General Manager, Furniture Division
Bro-Dart Industries
Montgomery, Pennsylvania

MISS REIMERS:

There are many popular uses of testing today. Every time you turn on a television set you are sure to hear about testing, test results, and laboratories in connection with everything from stomach to teeth. It is a very popular approach. Testing in laboratories seems to be the authority upon which we now rest.

Testing laboratories are divided into two types. One type is the commercial testing laboratory, and the other is one such as Buyers Laboratory. Commercial testing laboratories generally test to given specifications. A consumer goes to them and says, "Here are three pieces of equipment. I have to buy one and I want them all tested. Here are some tests methods I have found, and you are to use these methods." At Buyers Laboratory we go about things quite differently. First, we initiate testing. No one ever comes to us. We decide what should be tested from the questionnaires we send out to people to find out what they really want. We decide what should be tested, and then we go about testing it.

First, we decide on a category. When we began, things were simple. We started with copiers. Then we went on to electric typewriters and adding machines. With electric typewriters we had no real problems. There is a variety of electric typewriters, but as long as they have carriages of the same length, testing them is like testing apples and apples. Testing adding machines is not quite so simple. Adding machines are available with various controls and with various capabilities. Thus, one of the things we do at the laboratory is to make sure we get machines that are comparable.

Once we have purchased the machines, we go ahead and perform our tests. When I say we test all electric typewriters, I mean we test every machine on the market in this country that has any kind of distribution. When two typewriters are taken to a commercial laboratory for testing, generally the laboratory can only make comparisons between those two machines. We emphasize comparative testing because we believe it is extremely important.

A commercial laboratory is paid for testing. No one pays us for testing anything. No one comes to us and says, "You test this machine and we will pay you X dollars." Instead, we decide what to test and then distribute the charges among many people, each of whom pays a portion. If you are familiar with testing, you know that the costs are high.

Buyers Laboratory takes a different approach to testing. We think that it must be comprehensive; we do not accept other people's ideas. Some time ago we decided to test steel desks. (In fact, most of the equipment we test is steel. We have not yet tested wood furniture.) We must evaluate many aspects of furniture such as how big the top should be, how many drawers there should be, how big the pedestal should be, how high, and what should be on the top.

After we decide which particular models we are going to buy, we purchase them on the open market, usually at list prices. This is not to say that Buyers Laboratory has not been invited to use machines or to take vast discounts on all types of equipment. However, we cannot and do not do this. We buy just the way you do. Sometimes we go to distributors and buy blind to make certain we are not getting anything that is "souped up" or special.

Testing is a peculiar and an expensive process, and, unfortunately, it can be both good and bad. We try to make sure that it is good. Testing must have a meaning. If you hit a typewriter with a mallet ninety-four times and beat another typewriter an equal number of times, in the end you have comparative results. But what do these results mean? Actually, they do not mean much. How many people pound a particular spot on a typewriter with a mallet?

There are also types of testing which simulate but are not exactly like actual use. Value testing comes somewhere in between. One of the most important things we do is to make sure we do have value testing. When we look for test methods, we start with GSA [General Services Administration]. There are various organizations that have test methods. Not everyone has them. Currently, there are no satisfactory tests for electric typewriters. There are test methods for various items of furniture but no tests for offset duplicators, postage meters, or other items that really need testing. For this reason we must often devise our own tests.

When we test, we break the procedure down into various aspects. One test we use is the durability or life test. This means that we take typewriters and subject them to 630 hours of typing. This is roughly 20,000,000 characters, which is the equivalent of one-and-a-half to three-and-a-half years of heavy to light use.

We take file cabinet drawers and push them in and out, as in the federal specifications, with 64 pounds for 50,000 cycles. What happens to that drawer? Does it fall apart, or does it continue to work? What is the pressure required to open and close that drawer at 10, 20, or 50,000 cycles? We cannot tell you exactly how many years of wear this equals for a file cabinet, because we do not know. We estimate, however, that this is from ten to fifteen years of normal use.

If we test up to 5000 cycles (630 hours) on a typewriter, we have more confidence in our measurements. We know this is equal to from one-and-a-half to three-and-a-half years of use, and, as a result, we can tell what is likely to happen to your own machines within that time.

We conduct what we call a pounding test on adding machines. This differs from the pounding tests done on typewriters. For adding machines we use an automatic, type B machine. We use American automatic typewriters and pull from underneath or push from the top, depending on the machine we are testing. This particular testing machine runs on a piano-type roll set up with standard typing patterns on the typewriters and adding machines. This is the same kind of use the machines would receive in an office. We cannot do the same kind of testing on other types of equipment.

In testing offset duplicators, for example, we have not yet found a way to load paper automatically. An electrostatic copier can be set for so many copies, but after five hundred sheets the paper supply has to be replenished. There are many things that can be done automatically, but there is no way to speed up the testing as we do it on typewriters for a life test.

Many people think the life test is the be-all and end-all of testing. It is vital to know how long a machine is going to last, but there are other aspects of performance that must be checked on any kind of machines. It is all very well to have a typewriter that is not going to break down for at least five years, but what is the typewriter going to do? Is it going to do the kind of work that is needed? Is it going to type as many carbon copies as needed? Is it going to have half spacing? There are peculiarities of every machine that need to be checked. Will the typist have to

reach an extra inch to find the carriage return? Are the control keys on the adding machine located so that anybody can find them? Are they marked or unmarked? Is the adding machine one that can be used by almost anyone, or must it be used by a skilled operator?

In addition to durability testing, therefore, an engineering examination is usually necessary. We also concentrate heavily on performance testing: What does the machine do? Even if it is a desk, what does the desk do? If all you need is a desk top, almost any desk will do, as long as you do not sit on it or spill things on it, but if you need more than a desk top, then there are other points you should look for. This is partly performance testing and partly a different type of testing. When you open the drawers, do you cut your hands? This may sound silly, but we test for that. We take cheesecloth and run it across all the edges and the hardware with which you are going to come in contact. Is it going to stain when a cigarette ash or a cup of coffee is dropped on it?

What typewriter should you buy? To find the answer, we have a battery of typists who go through all the standard typing procedures. They type standard patterns with so many carbons of a certain type. We want to know how good the carbon copies produced by a given machine are. We try to test for the total performance of the machine.

We do durability tests on ballpoint pens. That is only one part. We also give pens to a dozen people and ask them to write with them. What is the performance of the pen? Does it skip? Does it stop? We make notes on the performance. We test offset duplicators. We test postage meters. How easily do they work? Where are the controls? Do they perform as they should?

The final aspect of our testing is a survey. Every time we test we buy only two or three samples of any given model. We are not the richest laboratory in the world, and the capital expenditure involved in buying and testing half a dozen of each model typewriter on the market is rather high, so we only test two or three samples. If we find discrepancies, we will buy more. If we have any reason to believe that we are getting duped, we buy under an assumed name. We usually buy furniture under an assumed name or through a distributor.

In order to have a controlled test, we do a survey. We phone people, write people, and go out and see people. We receive information from people who have from 100 to 10,000 pieces of any given type of equipment, people who have hundreds of typewriters, including possibly a few hundred IBM's and a few thousand Underwoods. These people constantly feed back information about what these machines are doing and what kind of breakdowns they have. We compare these results with those we get from the laboratory. If we see that a gadget is breaking down on machines in the field, that is one thing. If the gadget is not breaking down on our machine, our machine may be better; if the gadget breaks down fourteen times in the laboratory but no one in the field has trouble, it may be that we have a lemon. In that case we go out and buy an additional sample.

As soon as we identify a machine we are interested in testing, we talk with the salesman and find out as much about it as we can; then we talk with the manufacturers. When we have a rough draft of our testing report on the machine, it is sent to the manufacturer. He is then free to refute what we have found. We feel that a manufacturer has a great deal to offer so we give him every chance to prove that his product is acceptable. He can go outside our company to find out what other people have to say about the product. If he can find fifty people who have not had a problem with it, perhaps our test method is wrong.

Next, the draft reports are distributed to the staff, and everyone reads and criticizes them. Eventually we publish a report in a slightly different format than that of Consumers Union. We do not charge on a project basis; we charge on a subscription basis, very much like *Consumer Reports*.

As a matter of fact, the man who started *Consumer Reports* started our company also, so we have a background of consumer-type testing, i.e., testing for the user as opposed to testing just the machine itself. There are many kinds of testing. Durability testing of the type we do is difficult. It is also expensive. When we tested copiers some years ago, it cost us about $40,000. Just to do the durability testing on typewriters, counting equipment and man hours, costs $10,000 to $15,000.

Many of the big items of equipment are too expensive to be tested by either the individual purchaser or a commercial laboratory. There are some things, however, that the individual purchaser can look for. We do not advise anyone to go buy a couple of typewriters and test them himself. We do advise him to make sure before he buys a typewriter that he knows exactly what kind of work he wants it to do and that he take that kind of work and try it on the typewriter. This means that if he is going to do as many as fifteen carbon sets or manifold copies, he should take them down and try them on the typewriter or have the machine brought in on a demonstration basis. Little things have turned up, such as on the older Hermes typewriter, for instance, which had a carriage return key too far away. Typists often complained about the placement because it tended to slow down their speed. On this year's model the return key has been moved back so that it can be reached more easily.

We tested the Selectric, which happens to be one of the most durable machines we have ever found, particularly for automatic typing. The Selectric, or "gold ball" machine, was designed by IBM, and IBM is the only company that produces such a machine. It was probably designed for input to computers. For everyday use in the office, it is an excellent machine, but if one has to do many carbons, the best results are obtained using the special Selectric carbon papers.

Because catalog cards are so important to librarians, we are in the midst of testing various cardholding devices and platens on typewriters. If you are going to use a typewriter to do a lot of hard typing or to make many carbon copies, remember to look for hard platens. The type of platen makes a difference in the number of carbon copies that can be made.

As for adding machines and calculating machines, the user should know what type of work is to be done. Too often at the laboratory we hear of people with calculators who require nothing more than a multiplier or an adding machine for most of their needs. We hate to see people overbuy, just as much as we hate to see them underbuy. You do not really need a printing calculator unless you have to do interrelated problems, or division, or multiplication.

We have found a great deal of interest in electrostatic copiers among consumers. There are some eighteen or nineteen different copiers in various models.* We have tested most of them, but we still have a few more to test. Sometimes we cannot get a copier into the laboratory because the manufacturer will not let us have one. He knows we are going to test it and he is afraid of the results.

Many people tend to think of copiers as synonymous with Xerox; they are not. Xerox will give very high quality copy if the machine is kept in good condition. If it is not, Xerox will not produce any better copy than other machines. We find that copiers which produce the best quality are a well-maintained Xerox or a Bruning 2000.

A well-maintained Xerox makes good copies and a poorly maintained Xerox makes poor copies. If you do not maintain it, Xerox is not a machine you should have.

Bruning has two large, flat-bed, dry-toner machines: the model 2000, and another one, which is about to come out. Both are excellent machines and make good copies. The problem with the Bruning is that there are minor details that can go wrong with it. It does not have to be maintained as carefully as the Xerox, but it does have to be repaired. However, it is not a difficult machine to repair. If you want top quality and do not want a Xerox for some reason, this is the machine to consider. Bruning is also coming out with a flat-bed copier based on a different principle. The other two machines are dry toners. This will be a wet toner.

*Since this speech was given, Buyers Laboratory, Inc., has tested a total of thirty-three copiers.

The Frantz machine is another small copier.* The last price we had on it was $995. The copy quality, however, is not spectacular, and it is not a machine we recommend.

I do not know what to say about the Xerox 813 except that it is a Xerox machine and that it has some trouble with feeding and delivery. It produces copy of good quality, but again it must be well maintained.

There are two types of electrostatic copiers: the liquid-dispersant type and the dry-toner type. The only dry-toner machines available now are the Xerox, the Apeco, and the Bruning. All others use a liquid-dispersant toner which will give a slightly grayer background than a well-maintained Xerox. The quality can be acceptable although it may vary sharply.

The Xerox company has a new plan. They will continue with their regular Xerox plans. They have an 813 and a 330. The one- and two-meter plan on the 813, the 914, the 420, and the 720 will continue in operation. When a certain volume is reached on all of these machines, they cut their prices drastically; they have cut them to the point where, if you make 120,000 copies a month on a 2400 you will be paying $1100 a month, or about a penny a copy. If you make over that number, over 120,000 a month, you will be paying a half a cent.

On the 720 the minimum is 36,000 copies. This machine is the 914 with three meters, and you will be paying $.0167 per copy for the first 36,000 copies. After that the price decreases to a little over a penny for the next few thousand copies. The minimum is what is important and it is given in terms of hours. With the 2400 it is about fifty hours; you can translate that into the number of copies. The figure may or may not be exact.

On the 914 there is a minimum of 6800 copies, which will bring the cost down to about two cents; on the 813, the minimum is 5000 copies, which brings it down to three cents. If your volume of copying is high, you have to decide whether to go to a combination copier and duplicator or to these Xerox copiers with the new payment plans. We are not yet sure how this works out financially, but still have doubts about using a copier married to a duplicator.

New machines we have received include the Apeco Super-Stat. This has a flat bed and a liquid toner. It is the only Apeco machine with a liquid toner.**

The Royfax machine, also fairly new, is a Litton Industries product and uses a liquid dispersant. However, it produces the best-quality copies of any of the liquid dispersant machines we have seen to date. We do not know the prices.

There are other machines that are in or that are coming in. The Smith-Corona 55, which is a large flat-bed copier, will probably interest some of you. We have not yet received it, but we have heard that the costs are very low. Copy quality is fairly good. We have tested other Smith-Coronas and have always found them effective. The copy quality is not the best, but it is always legible.

There are a few small inexpensive machines available. One is the Ditto, which now costs about $600. It is supposed to be the answer to a poor man's prayer; it may or may not be. So far we have had trouble with the originals jamming and then copies do not go in. The controls are not marked, so it is hard to figure out what to do. There is no paper guide, just a simple little gadget. The copy quality is not too good, and we are not favorably impressed with the Ditto machine.

Ditto also produces a machine under the Universal label. If a gear system is added and the performance improves, this machine, because of its low price, could be valuable. Right now we do not think it is the answer.

The cheapest machine available today is the Electric Copier 200, which is distributed through Kee Lox. This machine is very small, about the size of a bread box. In fact, it is the smallest electrostatic copier on the market. It is also the least expensive, about $300 or $400. It copies only one side of the original, and it is not a flat bed; it is a roller copier, so it cannot be used for books. It may be useful in a small operation as a replacement for a wet copier. Copying one side of originals cuts down its use considerably, but for other purposes it is all right.

Other machines we have tested include the Savin and the A. B. Dick machines, which are supposed to be exactly the same. Both use National papers and the same toners. Both are good machines. The problem we had with the Savin and the Dick was that A. B. Dick had better quality control when National delivered the paper for them. We had the feeling that if they sent paper to Dick and Dick rejected it, it was sent to Savin. The Savin machine is exactly the same as the Dick machine, and yet we get much better copies on the Dick than we do on the Savin, which points up that if you are having problems with the machine it might be well to check your suppliers. If you have a Savin and are having trouble with it, call Dick and see if they will sell you paper. Savin may have corrected this situation.

Some SCM machines are good. We recommend them for medium-volume operations where the use is likely to be limited.

---

*This machine is no longer manufactured.
**At the time of this speech, testing was still in process and the results inconclusive.

DISCUSSION

Question from the floor: Are coin-operated copiers recommended?

MISS REIMERS: I do not know anything about coin-operated equipment except when it is Xerox. If you maintain the Xerox, whether it is coin-operated or not, Xerox quality is good; if you do not maintain the machine, the poor quality is not the machine's fault.

Question from the floor: The Xerox takes quite a bit of maintenance, does it?

MISS REIMERS: Generally speaking, the 914's do, yes. There is a big selenium drum in the machine and it must be cleaned constantly. It should be cleaned about once a day or once a week. You take your choice and get quality depending on how much you baby it. There are other machines such as the Smith-Corona Marchant, the SCM 55, that have a flat bed, which I assume you need so you can copy books.

Question from the floor: Is the Dennison a fairly new one?

MISS REIMERS: Dennison is not new. It is a fairly good machine. Perhaps some people can tell us about their experience with a Dennison. Xerox is only one brand. Any of these other machines with flat beds are also possibilities. At Buyers Laboratory we are concerned about the cost per copy, but if you operate in such a way that you recover all your costs from your customers, then you may not have to worry about this problem.

Comment from the floor: Our principal problem is that we do not want to spend too much staff time on copiers. We do have other Xeroxes on the campus so they can be maintained together.

MISS REIMERS: If you have other machines and they are being maintained, that is fine, as long as you have someone who knows how to clean the drum and take care of the feed problems.

Question from the floor: Of all the different kinds of copiers, can you name those on which we can copy books? Most libraries do not want one designed to copy single sheets because of its limited usefulness. On which of those you named would we be able to copy a book?

MISS REIMERS: Those machines which will copy books are the Apeco Super-Stat and the Bruning 3000, as well as the new Bruning 2100. Then there are the Smith-Corona, or SCM Coronastat 55, and the Xerox 914.

Xerox has many meter plans. The 914 with one meter is called a 914; the 914 with two meters is called a 420; and the 914 with three meters is called a 720. They are basically the same machine except for the meters. For every copy made on the 914, X number of cents is charged. The first four copies of any given original made on the model 720 (the 914 with three meters) are charged at four cents. The fifth through the tenth copies of the same original are charged at three cents, and all copies over ten are charged at one cent. This model is advantageous only if five to ten copies of the original are made. If only one copy is needed, it has no advantage.

The Xerox 2400 looks like a dream copier, but look carefully into the costs before you buy. I also have a warning about the 2400. Although it is supposed to use any kind of bond paper, it has trouble feeding paper with lint on it. As a result, it should be used only with hard-finished or spirit duplicator type papers.

The Dennison has a flat bed. The 3M model 209 is not an electrostatic copier, but it should be included with those able to copy books.

Comment from the floor: The Vicomatic is a little machine with a piano roll. It is a flat-bed copier.

MISS REIMERS: This is the machine that is now produced by Underwood and called the Book Copier. We have not tested it.

Question from the floor: What about the Thermo-Fax?

MISS REIMERS: Thermo-Fax machines are not flat bed.

Response from the floor: There was one that was.

MISS REIMERS: That is a 207, or a 107, or a 209. Thermocopiers, such as the Thermo-Fax, produce copies on a thin paper. If you need to consider the weight of the paper on which the copies are made, these are not machines we advise. Thermocopiers also have the disadvantage of not being able to copy colors. The Thermo-Fax people, or 3M, make the little thermocopier which, if quality of copy is not a major concern, is a fine machine. They also make a large machine which produces the same kind of copy.

They make two machines with flat beds. One is the 107, in which a pink sheet is used, exposed to light, removed, and then put through again. Making multiple copies is not its best use. This machine has been redesigned and it is now called 209. It has been increased about three times the original size. Instead of a sheet of pink paper, a roll of pink paper is fed in and goes automatically from one side to the other before the copy comes out. Copy quality is fair, but the copy is hard to write on with a ballpoint pen.

Question from the floor: Can you give us some information on the electrical power required for various copy machines?

MISS REIMERS: We give power requirements in each of our laboratory reports. The only machine I can think of with unusual power requirements is the Xerox 2400 which takes 220 volts.

Question from the floor: In evaluating copiers do you differentiate between those designed for coin operation and those designed for normal operation?

MISS REIMERS: So far we have not differentiated between machines used for coin operation and those for individual or company operation. We have not had enough libraries write in and say, "Why don't you do it?" If anyone wants us to distinguish between them, he should write in and request that we do.

Question from the floor: Does an institution subscribe? Does it pay so much a month, so much a year, or may it simply purchase individual reports that are available?

MISS REIMERS: We sell subscriptions to the Buyers Laboratory reports for $135* a year. These come in six portfolios. If you are a member of AMS [American Management Society] or NAEB [National Association of Electrical Buyers], you can purchase the reports for $95.* We do sell individual reports from the portfolios of reports. If you are a non-subscriber, the cost is $45 each. We are not promoting this because we want to sell yearly subscriptions. Also, a yearly subscriber can buy all the back reports for about $50.

THE MODERATOR: The Library Technology Program of the ALA publishes *Library Technology Reports,* and these include some test reports from Buyers Laboratory. In the future the *Library Technology Reports* will contain more reports from Buyers Laboratory covering library equipment. The coin-operated Xerox 914, I think, is to be tested shortly. Meanwhile, I know there are some libraries that have used the machine with success. It does have to be maintained, but if there is another machine in the same building, it is not difficult to have the Xerox maintenance man service both machines at the same time.

Somebody asked about the Vicomatic. I have been told by librarians who have them that they have been generally satisfactory, but that there is a fairly high maintenance problem in some areas, depending largely on the service man. One area may have a good service organization and a library will have few problems, and in another area the service may be poor. You find out how good the service is in your area by trial or by talking to someone else in your general region. This copier produces a negative instead of a positive, which may influence your decision if you are interested in the Vicomatic.

*The subscription price is now $165; the price for AMS and NAEB members is $95.

MR. JACOBS:

The testing and value analysis I am going to discuss relates strictly to wood and wood finishes as applicable to library furniture. Library furniture is different from furniture in homes and from furniture in classrooms, for the following reasons: It is institutional furniture. It takes a lot of beating. Also, it is supposed to be aesthetically correct in the area in which it is placed. You may be satisfied with a simple, straightforward desk in a classroom of a school, but this simple, straightforward desk is not what you as librarians, or architects, or consultants are looking for in a library; you are looking for a combination of aesthetics and durability.

You must understand the interrelationship between wood and wood finishes because they cannot be separated. Many books and periodical articles suggest that one wood or another may be used strictly for aesthetic appeal, and that this or that finish should be used for durability. The function of a wood finish is twofold: first, to protect the item; second, to enhance its appearance. You can take a panel or natural wood, either plywood or solid lumber, and finish it without using a stain over it and get one characteristic. Take the identical piece of wood, perhaps half of the same panel, apply a particular stain to it, and you have an entirely different appearance, and possibly a difference in the characteristics of that finish insofar as protection is concerned.

There are few adequate performance tests for raw wood itself, and, as had been mentioned, the more the amateur tries to specify criteria for wood processing, the more likely he is to get into trouble. One of the things manufacturers have against this type of specification is that unless they are willing to go all out and change from procedures that have proven satisfactory to them, they are not going to be able to conform to the specifications. If they do, the product is going to be substantially more expensive and possibly, no matter how carefully you research the subject, not as good. Indeed, some manufacturers simply refuse to change to different procedures.

Virtually every species of wood is available. There is nothing to stop you from specifying knotty pine if that is what you want. Nor is there anything to stop you from turning to the manufacturer and saying, "What do you suggest? What do you recommend? Why?"

There are two groups of woods from which to choose: First, are the close-grained woods or hardwoods, such as northern hard maple and birch. These two may be used interchangeably; indeed, in certain cuts even experts are fooled by these woods. Also in the hardwood category but with an open grain is the old standby oak, which is suitable and certainly durable. Technically, a close-grained wood is desirable because it establishes a solid foundation for a stain or color on which the top coat may be applied. The fruit woods, such as cherry and others, may fall into this category because of color or grain, but in the case of fruit woods neither of these increases the durability of the top coat.

The second major classification is the exotic woods, such as teak and rosewood, both used recently in some large library installations. There is a difference between oak and maple, but there is a more substantial difference between oak or maple and rosewood or teak. The exotic woods have another desirable quality, which is probably the primary reason for choosing them, and that is they are different. They are aesthetically desirable, but the same people who recommend fruit wood do not take into consideration the characteristics of this raw material and its performance after being in use three, four, five, or fifteen years. How has fruit wood rated in terms of maintenance and how has the product itself stood up as the result of this top coat?

The standard library furniture specification today usually reads "close-grained hardwood." It may mention, and usually does, birch or maple. We have seen a profusion of walnut recently, although it is becoming more scarce. Walnut has been used in household furniture long enough that the supply has been severely reduced. It is certainly among woods that will take a finish well, and it does have some of the characteristics desired in a library. However, because the veneers cannot be produced or manufactured with proper thickness in comparison with the other hardwoods, and because the selection of the wood today does not measure up to what it used to be, walnut is possibly not quite as desirable as it has been previously.

Some experts or architects familiar with wood have used the exotic woods successfully. I have seen several installations where teak has been used, but most of them did not work out as successfully as they might have otherwise. The finishing of these exotic woods is a special process. They do not lend themselves to the mass production methods commonly used in the furniture industry today. I say this not because you cannot have what you want or what you think you want, but because you must be aware of the overall situation in the marketplace today as viewed by consumers, architects, and manufacturers.

The library furniture market has grown tremendously, and thousands of dollars have been spent in an attempt to keep pace with the increasing demands for its products. What happens when a contract specifies a unique wood or a unique finishing procedure? The buyer, the customer, can force compliance to the specifications; he can reject anything that does not meet the specifications precisely. But how can you force compliance to those specifications?

Therefore, when considering use of an exotic wood or a departure from a standard item, think about the additional cost which will surely result and what it means to the manufacturer in relationship to other business potentially available to him. The library community is a relatively small one, and, with few exceptions, the manufacturers of library furniture are not involved with other items. As a result, a gamble on an untried or untested specification which does not turn out well reflects directly on that manufacturer.

Thus, manufacturers are prone to use products and methods they have tried and tested themselves. The close-grained hardwoods are suitable for a specific technical characterization and as a base for durable furniture and a durable finish. The deficiency of a close-grained hardwood, if it can be called a deficiency, is that it is commonplace; everyone has it— high schools, schools, public libraries, big colleges, and small colleges. Therefore, your consultants or your architect may say, "I want to do something different. I don't want to follow along. I don't want what everyone else has." This is probably the main reason we are attempting to use different species of woods.

The species of wood is important. The wood finish is equally important. Unlike wood itself, the finish does lend itself to performance tests. If we choose a different type of raw material—a wood species other than a close-grained hardwood—we are going to have different specifications, a different method of application, and a different result than we would with the close-grained hardwoods such as birch or maple.

The finishing procedures used most commonly on close-grained hardwood are as follows:

First, the material to be finished must undergo a standard finishing procedure. A proper standard does not mean just passing over it with a machine. Nor does it mean overconcentration on enhancing it. It means sanding it properly to remove the fibers from the wood to prepare that wood for finishing. One of many types of stains is then applied. It may be sprayed or wiped on. After the staining operation a coat or sealer is sprayed on. It does not seal the wood against movement. If wood is going to move, it will move. The sealer merely prevents the color from changing when the top coat is put on or from bleeding into the top coat. After the sealer the piece is again sanded. Following the sanding operation, one coat of the top protective coating is applied. After a short period of time, a second sanding operation may follow and usually one more top coat is applied. After drying, whether air drying or oven baking, the piece can be hand-rubbed to produce the finish which is required on so many specifications. Following this, the piece is waxed, which improves the quality of the finish insofar as the durability is concerned.

Let us look at this operation again and see what it means from the technical point of view. How will a stain that is wiped on affect the durability of the finish? Anything that is wiped on and then wiped off—unless the piece is thoroughly clean, free from any residue whatsoever—will reduce the adhesion between the wood itself and the top coat. A piece of furniture may be magnificently constructed, but if the staining process was not carried out perfectly, the result will be ordinary furniture, which will not wear well. If the furniture will be in an area where it will make an impression on the patrons of the library, the type of stain is certainly important and the type of staining process is equally important. There is no performance test that you as a buyer can perform on a finish sample, which you may require with your bid, to determine if the stain itself is causing a loss of adhesion between the top coat and the wood itself. You cannot determine whether or not the top coat is adhering to the material you have purchased.

Top coats have been discussed widely in recent years, and a brief understanding of them is important. First, there is the old lacquer finish. This is nothing more than a simple protective, top-coating material which has the unfortunate characteristic of yellowing rapidly and becoming relatively brittle. There are later developments, however, which make this one of the very best finishing materials. It is very, very hard. The time spent to hand-rub items finished with it is usually excessive, but a good surface can be achieved that is not brittle and does not retard color change to any great extent. There are newer finishes such as conversion varnishes. These varnishes have the advantages lacking in the lacquer finishes. They are not brittle. Some of them retard color change. They stand up under a great deal of abrasion.

Plastic laminates are also used for protection. Formica and Micarta are utilized on many products that are used in libraries. In these products the base wood is not of great importance because their exteriors are virtually applied to them. If a piece of walnut Formica is put on top of a piece of pine, the piece is supposed to look like walnut. The benefits, of course, are that it has durability, insofar as resistance to normal wear and tear are concerned. It does have certain drawbacks, however. One problem to be concerned about where laminates are used is what happens if the item is damaged.

In general, the following demands can be made of wood finishes, wood and plastic laminates alike. First, adhesion: How well is this top coat going to adhere to the product? Finish tests can give us an idea of how good the adhesion is and how good the surface is.

Second, abrasion: There is no sure guide to which test is really comparable to the use or abuse that a table surface suffers from the abrasion of books on it over five or ten years or that a charging desk's leading edge receives from contact with belt buckles and other objects. Third, color retention: If a library is furnished in one color and three years later a new piece of furniture is added, will the color have changed so that a piece of the original furniture must be submitted to the manufacturer to be sure that the color will match? Even if that is done, will the material that the manufacturer is using then age and change color at the same rate as the material that the same manufacturer supplied three years before? Fourth, consider resistance to the action of maintenance compounds. We can all develop tests for resistance to lye. We can develop a test for resistance to sulfuric acid, but are we going to find these compounds used in the library? Is the library one in which a girl is going to paint her nails? Is it one in which she is going to put on lipstick and possibly leave a lipstick smear? These are applicable hazards. A heel mark from a black rubber heel is another one.

There are many tests available. These tests, like statistics, can be made to show almost anything a manufacturer or a purchaser wants them to show. I am not saying that a test can be rigged. I am not suggesting that a manufacturer might falsify a test, because if he does his actions will be discovered later. However, I can show you that plastic will stand an abrasion test beautifully, and I can also show you that plastic finishes under certain circumstances can stand an impact test better than wood finishes. But, under the use requirements to which this material will be put, there is a best method and a best test for each one.

Some people have referred to the tests of the American Society for Testing and Materials. Others have used federal test specifications such as those of the General Services Administration. No matter which tests are used, there can be variation within the same species of wood or variation in the same finishing material applied in exactly the same manner at different times. Therefore, test results on wood are not conclusively indicative unless a wide enough range of material is used, with attention given to the length of time the material has cured and the atmospheric conditions under which the product was finished.

There are new finishes available for close-grained hardwoods, but they are not in manufacturing specifications yet because the manufacturers are unwilling to adopt something as a standard practice without adequate testing and experience. No manufacturer is willing to go to a professional testing laboratory and get test results on an untried process. He wants to be sure. He may, over a period of a year or two or three, use several small orders to experiment, knowing that if anything goes wrong, the material can be replaced, if necessary, and the customer will not suffer as a result. He will experiment because he believes that there is no expedient method of testing for a proposed change in wood finish in the laboratory or elsewhere outside of actual use. Should the item deteriorate or break down, the finish will be the first thing the customer, the librarian, and the architects who may visit this installation will see. It is the first thing that will reflect upon the manufacturer and limit his ability to sell in the future.

If there are no sure tests that you as purchasers potentially or actually can apply to a product, by what then are you to judge? Basically, it is the integrity of the manufacturer. It has taken the manufacturer himself a long period of time to determine what will do the job, what will protect the product, what finishing procedure, what finishing materials, and what tests he can apply to assure that quality standards are maintained all the way through. In doing so, he separates his items into their particular functions. He can decide what the best materials for finishing are, but no single product is best in all instances.

I am not talking only about wood finishing. I am talking about the selection of plastic laminates, for instance, for use in specific areas in the library. The leading edge of the charging desk is a good place to put plastic laminate because wood finishes, no matter how close grained they are, eventually are going to be marred by belt buckles or zippers. On the other hand, a plastic edge itself may be damaged. Thus, the manufacturer often faces a dilemma because one material does not provide all the answers. A wood finish may resist abrasion and impact and may stand up under all of the cleaning compounds used in the library and under most of the patron hazards. Yet its color retention or resistance to color fade may be very poor.

The things you should be concerned with are these: Instead of requesting a laboratory test which will simulate five years of color fade, see a five-year-old library finished according to certain specifications. Some manufacturers have their color samples stamped with a date and will not use these color samples six months or a year later because they realize that the samples are no longer representative of the actual color that they are maintaining as a standard finish. By seeing a library that is four or five years old, you also have a chance to measure the effect of abrasion on the tables. You have a chance to measure the effect that objects dropping on the tables have had. In other words, the performance tests that may be used on a wood finish may provide a general guide, but they cannot provide as good a guide as library use itself.

Manufacturers are always seeking a different sales approach or something new. As a result, those with facilities large enough and who are vitally interested in getting ahead will maintain a research and development program strictly on wood and wood finishes.

There are many combinations of stains and types of sealers that can be tried and that are being tried every day by every large manufacturer of library furniture. Finishing is an operation separate from manufacturing, and it cannot be judged by a piece of equipment set to the proper tolerances. It is a matter of professional judgment to produce the uniformity of color and uniformity of film thickness to protect the top coat. Every one of these factors combines with the absolutely uncontrollable atmospheric conditions, particularly humidity. All of these factors make a difference in the final finish of a product.

You can go ahead and specify anything you want insofar as the commercial product and a method of application is concerned, but if the man behind that spray gun does not do the job the same way he did it when the plans were approved, you are going to get a basically different product.

I would like to take issue at this time with the position taken by the federal government that you can, through a specification or thorough inspection, eliminate the unsatisfactory. This may be true insofar as assurance of dimension or a particular construction feature, but these factors alone do not determine quality. For wood finishes, there is no positive way to check adherence to the finishing specifications.

Adherence to the performance test put in a specification can be checked. But performance tests representative of actual use in finish tests on two pieces of wood will show different results, in some cases because they were finished in the identical manner but under different atmospheric conditions. I myself have submitted several samples at different periods of time to commercial testing laboratories with specific federal-test lab specifications, and the results of those tests on one sample were significantly different from the results on the other sample. The materials used were identical, and the same person did the spraying operations in all three cases. One was done under the condition of low humidity and the other was done under the condition of high humidity. All these pieces of wood came out of the same pattern.

Thus, the ultimate safeguard is reliance on the integrity of the manufacturer, combined with an understanding of what the finish is supposed to do, what you want it to do, and what you are not concerned about. If, for instance, you are going to select your furniture with a dark finish, you may not be interested in the relatively fast color change of some of the otherwise excellent materials available today. If, on the other hand, your selection is to be made in the light color, you obviously do not want something that may turn color rapidly. In relying on a manufacturer's tests and specifications for a given product, you are depending on his experience, the equipment he has, and his integrity.

The manufacturer's integrity is simply a result of his desire to remain in business and to move forward in his business. He knows he cannot do it by supplying a product with a finishing material which may be less expensive, but which will not give good results over a period of time. Library furniture is different from household furniture. It is different from commercial furniture in that it is not manufactured in the same volume. Although the manufacturing operation itself leaves room for a certain standardization, the finishing operation is an art as opposed to a science. A machine can be set and possibly the nozzle on a spray gun can be set, but if the operator moves that spray gun a little more slowly or quickly one time than the next, different finishes will result.

Now, let us consider the actual locations, the areas where certain types of finishes should be used and can be used. Plastic laminates resist abrasion excellently and impact fairly well. One drawback, of course, is that they simply cannot be repaired easily. A piece of plastic can be stripped or cut out and replaced with great difficulty; but the result is certainly not a new product, does not look like a new product, and will not provide satisfaction. If the plastic is damaged as a result of some sharp object being ground into it—purposeful abuse—that scratch will last the life of the item. Plastic has some other advantages. It provides relief from wood that is often prevalent in a library. Plastic has been used successfully to achieve an aesthetic effect in the children's area of a library, where the desire for multicolored tables is combined with that for resistance to abuse.

On the other hand, wood is perhaps regarded as a more sophisticated material than plastic, and it has the warmth, beauty, and depth that plastic lacks. As a result, wood finished properly is commonly found in the adult areas of libraries on exposed shelving and front panels of charging desks and card catalogs.

We have seen a combination of wood and plastic on the same charging desk—a wood front and a plastic top, the plastic top bearing the abrasion the charging desk receives better than wood. In many cases in which plastic has been used in conjunction with wood, it was used in color, not in matching wood grain or in an attempt to camouflage the fact that it is plastic. The physical advantages of one combined with the design capabilities of the other add up to an attractive combination.

There is no one best way and no one best product. This can be proven by the number of library furniture manufacturers who are constantly experimenting, constantly going to different vendors of finishing materials and asking them to help solve the problems of durability and of the basic function of any wood finish, that is, the protection of the material beneath it.

In summary, I would like to consider first, what is it you want in your library? Are you more concerned with design and appearance than you are with durability and cost of maintenance? If this is the case, there is nothing wrong with using some of the exotic woods to achieve this design feature. If you are concerned with durability, if you are concerned with longevity of a product combined with minimal maintenance, then your choice should be the relatively close-grained hardwood species.

In considering all of these factors, I cannot emphasize too strongly the importance of consulting a reliable manufacturer on the qualities of the product and how it can be related to the development of the library you want to build. As we have seen and as I can demonstrate, tests are fine as far as they go, but tests must be suitable for the particular functions or the particular problems you are going to encounter.

It is interesting to note that although you can have these new and relatively advanced finishing materials applied to library furniture, it is exceedingly difficult in many cases to get a supply of chairs finished the same way. It is likely in the library, therefore, that you are going to get chairs finished one way and tables finished the other and that what will appear identical may only be the top coat. Possibly it is the sealer that shows the difference or its durability, and the durability may change.

Finally, I would like to discuss the study by Frazer Poole of finish tests related to his particular library program and how he solved the problem inherent in that program. He was concerned about certain criteria and functions that the wood finish had to perform and what dangers he might encounter in the selection of wood and finish that he finally specified. How did the tests protect him against the dangers of some of the finishes? He did it in the way I would recommend: He decided first what he wanted the product to do; second, what type of equipment he was going to have; and third, what colors it was going to be. On that basis many major manufacturers will be available to help by discussing the strengths and the weaknesses of the various finishes to assure adherence to the product.

DISCUSSION

THE MODERATOR: Let me refer to your last comment. The tests that we used at the University of Illinois, published in the April 1965 issue of *Library Trends*, were not new tests. They are widely used by the furniture industry as well as by government and by many private organizations. For the most part, they were tests developed by the American Society for Testing and Materials. They have been used over a long period of time, and I think they can be used in many situations to establish a minimum quality for finishes.

The point was made earlier that librarians should not try to specify the way wood should be finished or the staining procedure. This statement points out that librarians should not try to specify materials and methods if there is a better way to do it. When you take the specifications of a given manufacturer for materials and methods, you are pointing the finger at that particular manufacturer, thus making it very difficult for other manufacturers to conform to the particular specifications that you use or causing them to change their methods. In changing their methods, they may change the quality.

I do not agree that performance specifications are not useful. Performance specifications or performance tests are open to some objections. They are not perfect. Yet they are far better than no tests at all. I think most of us would like to be able to depend entirely on the integrity of the manufacturer, but we would be deluding ourselves if we did so. In fact, the success of organizations like Consumers Research and Buyers Laboratories is proof of the fact that the integrity of the manufacturer is not the only factor to be considered in purchasing equipment. We would be remiss, indeed, to purchase library furniture without attempting to assure ourselves by the best means open to us that we get the quality for which we pay.

You do not have to go far to see situations in which finishes are poor or places where construction is inadequate. The idea of going into a library that has been furnished for five years and inspecting the quality of furniture is a good one, but you should be very sure when you order furniture that the manufacturer uses the same procedures today that he did five years ago.

Finishing procedures do change, sometimes very rapidly. Thus, a four- or five-year test, or even a three-year test, for a finish may or may not be adequate. We must continue to do the best we can to assure ourselves that we get the quality we need. None of the methods we have talked about is perfect, and there are some ways in which these methods can be improved, but I would certainly not discard performance testing.

MR. JACOBS: One set of performance tests will not protect you in every specific situation, because no single finishing material will provide a perfect answer to all of the possibilities for failure. All of the requirements in your library program, including finish color, location, and function of the item, will determine performance tests applicable to your situation. Once those factors are determined, and you find a manufacturer whose product meets these particular performance tests, and you can see through examination of older installations that the performance test is applicable to that product, then that finishing procedure should be in your specification.

I do not believe in a single rigid set of performance specifications applicable to all finishing materials or all finishing material requirements.

Question from the floor: In Florida we have a humid climate. Are there special finishes or special products for different parts of the country?

MR. JACOBS: Yes and no. The answer lies basically with standard manufacturing methods and standard equipment, which produce top-quality wood finishes exactly the same for use under normal conditions. Many manufacturers, knowing that they are going to ship products into areas of high humidity, will change or alter their manufacturing tolerances for the items. Yet there is no assurance that difficulties will not occur. Woods do move.

There may also be a little bit more care, a little bit more of the sealer material sprayed on the items going into an area of high humidity. Hopefully, this will reduce or limit the amount of movement, but it does not always work out that way. Usually, insofar as the top coat is concerned, there would be no difference in the finishing between material going to Florida and that going into the mountains of Colorado, unless the architect specified it.

Question from the floor: You spoke of color fastness. Is this improved by choosing a color as close as possible to the natural color of the wood?

MR. JACOBS: This question leads off into types of stains. If you choose a natural finish and use a lacquer as opposed to some of the newer materials, such as a conversion varnish, the lacquer will yellow and the entire product take on a yellow cast. If you take one of the less expensive stains and spray walnut, for instance, on a piece of solid maple, that stain can turn into a red color and actually fade almost completely. You are not necessarily safe in choosing a color close to natural unless all of the other steps are covered as well. Once again, the manufacturer's responsibility and performance in the past regarding coloration and protection are the ultimate deciding factors. If a manufacturer has a product which you have seen time and time again and it has not been color fast, it is safe to assume this is something you do not want to use. On the other hand, if a manufacturer has products installed that are several years old and that seem to have retained their color and life, these are the products that you will want to use, regardless of the color applied to it.

Comment from the floor: In discussing some of the commonly used close-grained hardwoods—the northern hardwoods, maple, birch, beech, and elm —one point that was brought up was that one of the primary reasons for going to the exotic woods was that the close-grained hardwoods have become commonplace. I think there are other good reasons for not using the close-grained hardwoods.

One of their primary visual deficiencies is a lack of strong grain characteristics. From any distance at all, a wood such as white maple given a natural finish may look very much like any other wood finished with a beige paint. I think that the generally accepted characteristics of wood do not show up strongly in the close-grained hardwoods. There is another value to what are termed the exotic woods, and that is that many users of libraries and other similar facilities associate close-grained hardwoods with institutional equipment and treat the equipment as such. They tend to associate many of the exotic woods more with residential or other types of environment, and this association tends to bring about a greater respect for the material among the users.

Short supply was mentioned as one problem in raising the cost and in using some of the exotic woods. Walnut is probably the most commonly used of the exotic woods. The problem with the walnut supply is not that the walnut has been used so extensively in residential furniture, but the fact that over half of our walnut is being exported. If we used our walnut here rather than shipping it abroad, I think it would be available at not too much difference in price from close-grained hardwoods.

In purchasing furniture for libraries, watch very closely for such terms as "walnut finish." This almost invariably means a walnut stain on a close-grained hardwood, which to anybody but the most uneducated can be spotted a mile away. It does not bear any resemblance in color to walnut or to any other darker wood which the stain is to match. Be extremely careful in combining this "walnut finish" with a walnut-finish stain, or with any other darker stain on a close-grained hardwood, with a plastic laminate which is intended to match the walnut wood, because the grain characteristics of close-grained hardwoods are not extremely evident. The printed characteristics of the grain and the printed paper which forms the backup for a plastic laminate are a reasonably accurate reproduction of the more exotic wood. In color they are similar, but in grain characteristics they do not match at all.

Another point to watch for in combining any

wood with a matching wood plastic laminate is that all woods change color over a period of time; most dark woods will bleach and most light woods either gray or yellow and darken. Plastic laminates do change color, but they change very slightly. Five years after the purchase of a piece of equipment which is a combination of a wood-grained plastic laminate and a wood which initially matched it the two finishes may be quite different.

With respect to some of the catalytic lacquers, or conversion varnishes, and the epoxies, consider whether these materials are field reparable. Most of them are not. They require very close supervision of the application processes in the factory. Most of them also show scratches and minor abrasions rather distinctly because they have a tendency to chalk when they are scratched.

Another point to consider is the gloss factor in most of these catalytic finishes. A reduction in gloss in these finishes generally means some loss of durability of the finish. The degree of loss may vary, but the fact is that in going from a high-gloss finish to a low-gloss finish, some degree of durability will be lost. There is some compensation in that low-gloss finishes do not show minor abrasions to the extent that high-gloss finishes do. There is also the important functional factor of the low-gloss finish for reader use.

The dependence upon the integrity of the manufacturer was again brought up. There was a statement made that wherever possible five years' experience in the construction of similar equipment should be a part of the specifications. I think this would automatically eliminate, particularly in wood library equipment, some manufacturers, who have entered this field within the last five years, who stand very close to the top of the list in integrity.

Some mention was made of the use of plastic laminate on a charge desk. While I would not hesitate for a moment to agree that the plastic laminate would certainly be a more durable surface than a wood veneer, I have seen numerous charge desks in which large areas of the kraft paper backing on plastic-laminate tops were visible. Plastic laminates do wear, particularly under such heavy use as on a charging desk. In fact, they may wear very quickly. Other materials of a more durable nature, such as stone and artificial stone, might be considered for this use.

Also, the statement was made that with most library manufacturers the finishing operation is an art and not a science, and I do take some issue with that.

MR. JACOBS: That is what I mean by difference of opinion. First, everything this gentleman says concerning the selection of the type of wood goes back to my statement that hardwoods are commonplace. I was saying, in effect, that the exotic woods are not commonplace and, therefore, they retain a design advantage.

When we talked about institutional equipment versus the aesthetic qualities of furniture used in the home and the fact that librarians would like to have these same qualities in their libraries, we were talking the same language, perhaps in different words.

In speaking of close-grained hardwoods, however, we are talking about durability and I do not believe that, with the possible exception of walnut with some specific finish, you can compare the durability of the wide range of exotic woods with that of close-grained hardwoods.

Many new finishing methods and materials have come on the market in the recent past. Some of you may be familiar with the word *polyester,* or *epoxy.* As far as I am concerned, despite the claims that have been made for this material, I am unwilling to have it used on my product until I have had much more experience in controlling its application and in evaluating its performance in institutional use.

We do believe that the best furniture for wear is a piece that is made from close-grained hardwoods and finished with catalyzed lacquer, or conversion varnish. I am less concerned with the difficulty of making field repairs to furniture finished with such materials than I am with the color fade, water damage, and other problems caused by the use of the older, less durable lacquer finishes. No products are perfect in all respects; they are deficient in one way or another. Some of these products will satisfy the most stringent requirements for use in your particular library, and some will not. You must determine what the problems are that the finishing materials to be used on your particular library job will meet.

The comment about the reduction in gloss is absolutely true, and here again we get back to integrity because there is almost no way for you to determine the manufacturer's form of the finishing material that he buys. It is possible to buy a conversion varnish, or a catalyzed lacquer, with a low-gloss yield. This does reduce the durability of every finishing material. It will not stand up to the same abrasion tests that this very same material with a high gloss will. Again, we go back to the integrity of the manufacturer, since it is possible to take finishing material without any gloss-reducing addition and produce a satin or low-gloss finish by hand-rubbing. This is the way it should be done, and this is the way it is done in a quality manufacturing operation. Just because an item has a satin

finish with a low light-reflectance factor does not mean that it has a cheap finish. A hand-rubbed effect not only minimizes scratches but the high-gloss finish is almost useless in the library. Although we might consider it theoretically a better finish insofar as durability is concerned, your readers will be unhappy if they are sitting at a table that is finished in such a manner.

There are many manufacturers who would like to get into this business who are people of high integrity. On the other hand, there is no substitute whatsoever, in an industry in which we enter into contracts of such magnitude, for the demonstrated ability of the manufacturer chosen to do a substantial library installation. It is possible to build a substantial volume, and to build a relatively large furniture operation, on the basis of smaller jobs. A company can be built on the experience gained in these less sensitive jobs. On the basis of this experience, a firm that has been in business for five or six years may be able to demonstrate to a potential purchaser that it has the equipment, the wherewithal, the ability, and the knowledge to do a job on a large library. This happens in relatively few cases because library furniture is a product entirely separate from home furniture. It is a product that requires specialization, a product that requires the ability and the equipment to work to tolerances previously unknown to the woodworking industry. Those firms that are successful today in the library furniture business have managed to do this.

Question from the floor: There was an inference made that the close-grained hardwoods do not have any character to them or are not distinctive in appearance. The exotic woods are not necessarily exotic because of flashy grain, but because of their relatively limited supply.

Mr. Poole has one of the fairly common close-grained hardwoods in his library, and I think it is probably as exotic in appearance as many of the woods that we are talking about. The same thing is true of birch, which is a common wood.

MR. JACOBS: That is a point I did overlook. You can make birch, for example, come close to resembling walnut with the proper stain application and with the wood or the veneer cut the right way. In referring to the fact that a piece of northern hard white maple looks like a paint job, let us talk about a piece of solid lumber, perhaps a shelf, or an upright panel, or even a certain type of veneer used in a pattern vertically exposed. With the proper treatment or proper selection of material and the proper specification, it is possible to make these close-grained hardwoods whiter and less distinctive, as far as appearance is concerned. However,

I am thinking of something more than just the grain structure in such woods as teak or rosewood, in which we are talking about a variation in color. If you take a piece of maple, for instance, and try to match it to a piece of varnished rosewood, you cannot do it. You will have to come up with one of the colors in that rosewood. On the other hand, if you take a piece of birch, you can accentuate the grain characteristics, and you can have what you want with the proper staining procedure.

Question from the floor: Can you establish a time-table in terms of plastic being long-lasting? What are we talking about, one year, ten years, twenty years? What are we planning for? What do you have in mind insofar as permanence is concerned? Is it as long as there is a finish on the top or as it continues to resist abrasion?

MR. JACOBS: Most performance tests, although they may attempt to simulate a period of time, cannot give categorical evidence that the equivalent of five years' wear has been produced. I cannot give you any idea of what this represents in terms of time. This is why I suggested the visit to existing libraries to see what has happened. Remember that such tests as the abrasion test are essentially relative. There is no way of coordinating most tests with actual use.

Those of you who are involved in large equipment programs are really bound by your responsibility to see installations of various manufacturers using various materials and to determine from your observations which of these is best. We do not attempt to say that any finish will stand up under normal use for a period of five years or ten years. All we can hope to say is that it will resist abrasion effectively, it will resist impacts effectively, or it will be relatively slow in color change.

Nobody can really define what normal use is. Is normal use an elementary school? Is normal use a high school library? Is normal use an adult area of a public library with relatively low circulation, as opposed to one with heavy circulation? I do not think that there is any effective measure of such use for coordinating with performance tests. Performance tests are artificially contrived methods of demonstrating how a product compares with another product within the same test range.

Comment from the floor: The question was really unfair. Our essential concern when we build a building is that the equipment going into it is anticipated to last the life of the building, which it frequently does. In a sense, you get that durability which is determined by thirty years' use, and I think it is unfair for the audience to consider it this way. It is not designed for that purpose. What is it designed for?

MR. JACOBS: You can take existing installations today and the furniture in them is still perfect. As a result of normal use, the finish could be completely worn off the charging desk, the table top, etc. On the the other hand, the same finish on the leg of the table, where there is no abrasion, is perfect. The purpose of the finish is to protect the surface of the material itself. You can actually observe the fact that the finish is taking the wear, and not the wood itself. The surface that is taking that wear, whether it is a wood finish or plastic laminate, is what absorbs the punishment. The basic piece of furniture may be perfectly sound, but the finish is worn and it does not make any difference whether we are talking about library furniture or a piece of marble, because everything wears to a certain extent based upon the amount of use to which it is subjected. Not to expect such wear is beyond reality.

Comment from the floor: There has been a failure to use domestic woods other than hard maple or birch. It was mentioned that good walnut is scarce; it is perfectly true that walnut is being exported overseas. However, if you look for good, clear, select maple or birch, you will find the same problem of availability, and you find the same problem in getting good oak or good ash. On the subject of finishes, I think we are doing too much imitating in getting something to look like something else.

For the woman who asked what can we do about finishes in the humid climates, I can think of nothing better than walnut with an oil finish.

Question from the floor: What about the use of elm in library furnishings? Is it expensive?

MR. JACOBS: Basically, any wood besides the standard close-grained hardwoods, such as birch or maple, used by the major library equipment manufacturers will be more expensive for the reason that rather than use it at the same time or as a result of the production of standard items, it must be a "special." As a result, costs are going to be higher. They are based not merely on the cost of the material itself. The manufacturer's cost structure in this industry is not based on one item at a time except in the case in which there is a special requirement.

If you specify an unusual kind of wood nine or ten months before your library is opened, the fact that the manufacturer is able to add the cost of the special material, plus a small percentage to cover waste, may enable him to run these items off at the same time as his production runs. This way he will reduce the excess cost. Generally, however, the request for unusual species of wood is going to result in increased costs, because we are talking about a totally different design item.

Let us say that there are 250 or 500 of this particular design and of this particular species of wood.

Such an order opens the door not only to other cost procedures on the part of the basic or standard library furniture manufacturers, but also to contract manufacturing which may or may not use the same techniques in arriving at the design required by the architect or consultant.

Question from the floor: I see some new plastic-laminate shelving on the market. We are using more and more plastic-laminate furniture today in kitchens and dormitories, and, apparently, it is working out very satisfactorily. I know that you do manufacture hard board shelving for economy reasons, and as far as I know this has worked out very well. I would like to have your opinion about the possibilities of using plastic laminates in boards for library shelving.

MR. JACOBS: The product to which you refer is strictly a low-cost shelving item and has many shortcomings insofar as potential use in a library. We found one kind of shelving with plastic on all sides, or at least on the top and the front edge of the shelf, that had many advantages. One of the relatively new plastic laminates has an extreme resistance to abrasion. I believe General Electric makes one such laminate. The result is a very durable product, a stable product, as far as movement is concerned, but joining becomes a problem because of resistance to flexing in the shelf and because of the weight of the item itself. You must delve into all the ramifications of the item in question.

If we are talking about a shelving upright, we should ask if it will bulge. Will we tolerate a shelf that will bow? This is the basis upon which to judge if it is acceptable. If it is acceptable, then the laminated furniture market will open up a new area. Some of the new plastic laminates have a very substantial place in a library, and we have seen an increase in the use of prefinished materials. Plastic laminate on flake boards, or plastic laminate over a lumber core, or plastic laminate over plywood—these do have a place and they are growing in use.

THE MODERATOR: Can you tell us anything about the so-called Lockwood process, or irradiated wood surfaces?

Comment from the floor: It is a new process that is still in the developmental stage. Some of the manufacturers are considering it. Basically, it tries to do what a product known as Densiwood does in a different manner. It hardens the wood itself.

THE MODERATOR: I am told it is being used in other types of furniture and that it provides a very durable surface, almost as durable as the plastics, and is extremely practicable.

This is a field which is complex and in which there are many problems and many possible answers. The manufacturers, the architects, the testing laboratories, are working toward the same end: to produce the best product for the money to be spent, taxpayers' money or private funds. The manufacturers are doing everything they can to improve their procedures and methods. The laboratories are certainly on the lookout, as attested by this preconference equipment institute, to learn about improved ways of getting better equipment. It is an unending process, and perhaps this is what makes it so interesting.

Testing and Value Analysis, Part II

DONALD WILLIAMS
Technical Services Director
Huntington Laboratories
Huntington, Indiana

Our subject covers the work we do in our laboratory to produce the best products we can. In going through the testing procedures, we have many things to keep in mind. One is that there are so many dollars to spend on so many products. Many of our testing devices are "homemade"; some of them are very, very simple. Then there are others for which we spend thousands of dollars, such as the electronic devices necessary to get exacting measurements on certain tests.

As individuals in a society that each year consumes vast quantities of goods purchased from various stores and manufacturer outlets, and as persons responsible for procurement for a particular segment of this society that uses large quantities of supplies and equipment purchased from various manufacturers and dealers, you are aware of the advantages of seeking the best possible products for your use. In these days of enlightened consumer knowledge, no company can continue to sell products at the lowest price and accompanying lowest quality. Value is being built into products by control and testing procedures. If you have chosen good, nationally advertised, reputable companies, you have learned to expect value in the products you purchase.

These are some of the reasons why we do not like "approval lists." A reputable company is able and willing to develop and to produce products that are usually far above the minimum standards of many of these approved lists. The usual tendency is to consider any product on these lists as equal, whereas some just barely pass the minimum requirements, while others are far above them. There is no assurance that all products shipped are the same as the samples submitted for acceptance on the lists. We feel the reputation of the company and its desire to continue to satisfy and serve are assurance enough of the quality of the products.

Products need to be long-lasting to reduce the high labor costs of maintenance and replacement. In our field, labor costs are considered to be 90 to 95 percent of the maintenance expense. Savings in low-quality products are more than eliminated by increased upkeep. To find the best, longest-lasting products, manufacturers need to maintain constant research and testing procedures.

Just what these quality control and testing procedures are will be the main purpose of this discussion. We can assure you that these companies are not using gold where iron would be entirely sufficient any more than they are not using iron where gold is needed. In other words, they are using the right raw materials to give you true value and are doing this by means of a great many testing procedures from the intricate to the relatively simple.

There was a time when a product may have been given only one test before it was marketed. This one test attempted to prove whether the product would be satisfactory for the task for which it was made. Often this testing was done by the consumer himself. For example, in purchasing an automobile, he may have had to stop and fix a flat tire or work on the lights before getting it home for the first time. Now individual components and many seemingly insignificant properties are carefully checked before a product is turned over to the consumer.

Tests can be divided into a few major categories. One could be tests on raw materials used in production of the parts and/or the finished product. In the case of the automobile, examples would be the tensile strength or flexibility of the metal used in various parts; the aging, heat, and wearing tests on the rubber used in the tires; and the drying characteristics of the paint.

Another category could be the physical or appearance tests of the part and/or finished product. This is how it looks in static position in front of you. The clarity of the windshield and glass windows, the shine of the chrome and the paint, and the angle of the headlight beams are also examples.

A final category could be the finished product in action. Road tests on the car, gas consumption of the engine, and the comfort of the seats are examples. Of course, there are cases of overlapping in these categories. Not all of these tests can be run on the final product. Much testing has to be on batches of the steel or rubber used with a known probability of the end product also displaying these specific test results. The actual strength of the steel pieces used in the particular car you buy or the wearing quality of the tires on the car cannot be tested, for these types of tests are run until failure occurs. You do not want broken springs and worn-out tires. I have always marveled how the 18,000 or so individual pieces that go into making a car can be assembled on the production line with very little testing on the line and then function so well with such few bad results. The answer, of course, is the pretesting of the components that make up the parts of the car.

There are numerous instruments and methods of measuring or testing for any one property. For the same property one instrument and procedure may work best for one type of product, but for another product another instrument and procedure may be better.

Standard tests have been developed through the years by technical associations of various industries. We follow the American Oil Chemists Society and the American Society for Testing and Materials. Their test procedures are specific, detailed, and reproducible in any laboratory using the specified equipment and chemicals. They are constantly reviewing and adding to their lists of tests as needs arise.

There are times when a company uses its own testing procedures and equipment until such a time as one of these associations develops and adopts a satisfactory standard test. As new ideas and new products are developed, new testing methods also need to be developed. We are constantly working with committees in these associations to add to their standard tests. In a few instances there are specific properties that have seemingly defied the development of standard tests acceptable to all concerned. Some of these have been considered for years with little success.

It is practically impossible to establish production of any product on such a tight control that all the test figures are kept at one particular reading. Consequently, minimum and/or maximum figures or plus and/or minus figures are usually established. In rare cases these slight variations may be noticeable by the consumer, but usually it takes delicate measuring devices to note these small differences.

In deciding on the final products or formulas for production, whole series of tests are run on numerous samples of both raw materials and finished formulas. The number of samples may run into the thousands before a satisfactory final product is chosen. Screening tests are run and the number of samples is usually quickly sifted down to a few. Then exacting tests are run on these chosen few before the final decision is made. After laboratory tests are completed, actual use tests are begun. Our own custodian may try it, or some of the office help may take it home. Some customers are often very willing to try a new formula, especially if it has a possibility of solving a particular problem. Sometimes samples are sent to a limited area of people to obtain their reactions. There is no one particular place to start in these tests,

so we will begin our discussion with the products as you first see them. Tests for liquid cleaners are almost entirely different from those for floor coatings, so we made that division in the presentation of the tests.

The first characteristic of a liquid soap or detergent that is apparent is its thickness as it runs out of the drum. Viscosity is the chemist's term for this, and he measures it by various viscosimeters. The Brookfield instrument is generally accepted as a standard test. The size of the spindle used, the running speed, and the temperature all can be varied to give desired readings. Standards are set up for comparative tests. Viscosity used to be a pretty good indication of how much actual soap was in solution. With the advent of synthetic detergents in 1945 and the introduction of thickening agents, viscosity has come to mean nothing in respect to the quality of a liquid cleaner. Now viscosity merely tends to give an aesthetic "body" to the product or an appearance of richness that may be misleading as to the actual cleaner content, if that is the sole purpose of the viscosity. Ease of handling and time of emptying a container are probably the main criteria for establishing a particular viscosity for a product. Once a specific viscosity is established, it can be a useful control test for establishing the accuracy of the ingredients used in the production and the effectiveness of the production controls. The Zahn viscosimeter used the principle that the thicker products take longer to run out of a standard-size container. The flow time gives the reading. Standard Gardner tubes have been established and viscosities can be compared to these standards. Each tube contains a progressively thicker liquid, and the reading is the alphabetical letter on the tube that matches the viscosity of the product tested.

The color next strikes the eye. Insignificant as the color may seem, it requires much attention. Eye appeal, which may help the product to sell, and stability of the color in storage are the two main concerns. Sometimes coloring is used to make the product distinguishable from others. Usually samples are stored in sunlight and heat to test the stability of the colors in the solution under extreme conditions. Once a color is chosen, the production is usually checked visually against a control bottle. Some industries, such as the paint industry, have electronic devices for measuring color. Standard color tubes, such as Gardner color tubes, are sometimes used.

The odor of a liquid cleaner, commonly a pleasing perfume, becomes noticeable when the cleaner is used. Perfumes are added for various reasons, such as to cover up the natural odor of the product if it is disagreeable, to give a refreshing deodorizing scent that will be present during the cleaning process and linger after the work is done, to provide aesthetic appeal, and to make the product distinguishable from others. Stability tests are similar to the color tests, but the nose is still the only "device" used to test for odors.

Dilution tests may be run on a cleaner to see how it is going to look when mixed with various kinds of water. One water source may have an average of eight grains of hardness, and another may have twenty-four to fifty grains of hardness. The amount of cloudiness or lack of cloud is reported for various dilutions in distilled water, eight-grain water, and 24-grain water.

When a cleaner is used, its ability to foam becomes evident. Foam does not help the cleaning procedure; and, there are times when it may be disadvantageous. Low-foaming detergents are necessary for automatic dishwashers, clothes washers, and the large, scrubber-type vacuum cleaners. Women like a high foamer for hand dishwashing, and high foamers are desirable for carpet and upholstery cleaners. One test that is used extensively throughout the industry is the Ross Miles foam tester. Allowing various detergent solutions to run down from a large pipette above into a pool at the bottom of the tube builds up a foam; then height measurements are taken. As in many tests, different dilutions of a variety of cleaning materials must be run before one is able to determine the relative foaming ability of any one of them. After a while, it is difficult to find a cleaner that will foam any higher or lower than another. Then there are standards with which to compare any other product.

A test that is perhaps as important to the consumer as any of the others is the solids or nonvolatile solids. This test assures that the consumer gets the amount of solid material that he pays for. A small amount of the cleaner is weighed out in evaporating dishes; then the containers are heated in an oven at 105 degrees C. for three hours. Volatile materials, such as water, are boiled away, and the soap or detergent solids remain to be weighed. Thus, a percent of solids can be obtained, and the consumer can be assured of receiving 40 percent soap when he purchases a 40 percent soap.

Another device used to check the solids and also the proper chemical content is the refractometer. A light source is bent through a prism and then through the liquid. The angle of the bending of the light rays is recorded and matched against a standard known angle to indicate the accuracy of the production liquid. Reputable companies automatically maintain a set amount of solids for each product and are constantly checking this to see whether the actual solids of the product are as announced or agreed upon. For instance, if you buy a product under a specific trade name, you will always receive the same amount of solids with each shipment, allowing for a specified plus or minus for the uncontrollable small variations. Usually, as much solid material as possible is dissolved in the product which still maintains a clear, stable liquid. Specific gravity tests help control the proper quantities of ingredients in a product. Water is used as a standard; then all other liquids are measured in relation to water as 1.000. Alcohol and many other organic solvents are lighter than water. Chlorinated solvents and most salt solutions, such as soap and detergent solutions, are heavier than water. The weight of a certain amount of the product as compared to that of the same amount of water can give the specific gravity, but a Westphal balance, which uses the principle of buoyance, is usually used. A lighter liquid; will not support as much weight as a heavier liquid; the fact that a man cannot sink in the Great Salt Lake in Utah is an example. There is such a great amount of salt dissolved in the water that the liquid is heavy enough to hold up a man's weight.

Soaps and detergents possess, in varying degrees, the ability to hold finely dispersed soils in suspension for relatively long periods of time. This soil-suspending property is useful in a cleaner because in the usual cleaning process there is a period of time before the soil can be washed and rinsed away. Poor soil suspension can allow the loosened soil to redeposit back on to the surface. Tests are conducted at normal-use dilutions in bottles or test tubes with a standard soil, usually iron oxide powder.

The test for neutrality, i.e., the acidity or alkalinity of a product, is known as a pH test. Numbers from 0 to 14 were arbitrarily chosen for the limits of pH with 7.0 as the middle or neutral point. Pure distilled water has a pH of 7.0, but most other aqueous liquids have a pH above or below 7.0. The pH test does not measure how much acid or alkali is in the solution, but the intensity or strength of the acid or alkali. Thus, one ounce of a product in a gallon of water may give about the same pH as one pound of the same product in a gallon of water. Some products are naturally mild and others are naturally strong. Mild alkalinity is between 7 and 10, and mild acidity is between 4 and 7. Hydrochloric acid is strong, while boric acid is mild and even safe for use in eyes. Caustic soda, or sodium hydroxide, is strong, while borax is a mild alkali. Mild cleaners should be used where possible, although when necessary strong cleaners can be used with proper caution.

Proper mechanical or abrasive action can usually help a mild cleaner do a satisfactory job with maximum safety to the surface to be cleaned. The strong acid bowl cleaners and strong alkaline drain openers are examples of strong pH products that need cautious use. Electronic pH machines are usually used for accurate measurement; pH papers are available for rough testing.

The surface tension test of a cleaning solution can usually predict whether it will perform satisfactorily. Water has a natural force called surface tension that makes water want to draw itself into a ball such as a rain drop. This makes it appear as if a film were over the surface. It gives lift to a floating object. Without it many objects would sink. This is part of the reason a needle can float on the surface of water. Of course, salt in the water would help more, as explained in the specific gravity test. A soap or detergent must lower this surface tension appreciably, usually from a reading of 70 on the Tensiometer down to around 30, so that the water can be freed to wet and penetrate into the smallest openings of the surface to be cleaned. Even a duck cannot float or swim in a cleaning solution. Thus the wetting and penetrating ability of a soap or detergent is also greatly improved by the lowering of this surface tension. A piece of cotton can float on top of water for a long period of time, but the addition of a little detergent will immediately cause the cotton to sink.

Emulsifying power is the ability of a soap or detergent to cause water to blend or mix or emulsify with oils, waxes, greases, etc. Once the emulsion is made, the length of time that it is stable is important because if the emulsion breaks or separates before the surface is rinsed, there will again be redeposition of the soil, which usually includes some oil, wax, or grease.

Cloud point is the temperature or temperatures at which a liquid product as it is shipped may become cloudy. This is important because once a product clouds, it usually separates into one or more layers. Some products will cloud at a certain temperature only while being cooled, possibly to 35 degrees F.; others will cloud only while being heated, possibly to 125 degrees F.; and others, interestingly, may have a cloud point both at a cool and at a warm temperature. Extremes of shipping and storage temperatures must be considered in the formulation of products.

Determination of the effects of freezing may be considered another test. Some products may cloud and/or freeze solid at below freezing temperatures, usually at 0 degrees F. Sometimes this freezing permanently damages the product, and sometimes thawing may leave the product in satisfactory condition, especially if it is stirred or agitated after thawing to make it uniform again. There are times when a product is damaged only after three freeze-and-thaw cycles on the same sample. Thus, the number of freeze cycles before failure is often reported. To be certain of the test, three or more freeze cycles are usually run on all products.

The most important overall test of a cleaner is its cleaning efficiency, or detergency test. This tests the ability of the cleaner to clean specific soils from various surfaces. Due to the complexities of soils and surfaces, this is one of the tests that so far has no industry-wide standard acceptance. Dishwashing detergents may be tested by counting how many soiled dishes a carefully measured dilution will clean before the cleaner is exhausted and the dishes do not become clean any more. Washing pieces or swatches of soiled cloth is a common test for laundry detergents. Painted stainless steel sheets and panels of common flooring materials such as vinyl and rubber are used as substrates or surfaces for testing. Various soils are applied to these surfaces and scrubbing is done by oscillating scrub brushes or sponges. There are numerous types of soil mixtures used. We like to use a blackened wax formula, especially for testing the abilities of our wax strippers. The attempt is made to simulate in a laboratory procedure a situation as close to the actual use conditions of a cleaner as possible.

There are many tests of an analytical chemistry nature that are not necessarily tests for the properties of a product, but that are used to test the presence of and the correct amount of one or more ingredients in a product. The gas chromatograph is used to sort out the ingredients in a column by means of intense heat and the results are recorded in graph form. Comparison with control charts can accurately assure the trained operator whether certain ingredients are present and whether the right amount has been used.

The colorimeter is also used for similar purposes. It may be more effective for one type of ingredient while the gas chromatograph may be more effective for another. Color changes are induced in the product being tested by the addition of proper chemicals. The intensity of the color is indicated on the electronic scale so that exact quantitative measurements can be made. Germicide content of disinfectant products and hexachlorophene content of bacteriostatic soaps are regularly checked by these tests.

Other analytical tests may be made using relatively simple chemical laboratory apparatus. The percent of ash is found by weighing the material first and then burning it in a crucible. The weight of the inorganic material which remains after this ashing makes it possible to determine the percent of ash. The amount of alkaline materials in the ash can be found by titration of the ash. Titration is the measuring of how much standard acid solution is necessary to neutralize or bring to a pH of 7 the remaining ash. A pH meter or a color indicator such as phenolphthalein may be used to indicate when neutrality is reached. Color indicators produce changes of color as acids or alkalies are added.

Alcohol dissolves certain ingredients and not others, so it is often used to separate the product into alcohol-soluble and alcohol-insoluble portions. Tests can be run on these separate portions to gain further information.

The alkalinity of the alcohol insolubles indicates the strength of the alkali, as well as the amounts, so that cleaning ability and possible harm to surfaces can be predicted.

Free oil is found by mixing petroleum ether with the product and finding how much, if any, oil is dissolved by the ether. Free oils can be harmful to some surfaces.

Soap products have certain tests peculiar to them. The free fatty acid or alkali test gives the amount of uncombined or unneutralized acid or alkali in the soap. This is a test of the purity of the soap. Another purity test uses a centrifuge to force any possible precipitate to settle to the bottom. Soaps should be precipitate free. The acid value or the amount of fatty acid gives the percent of unsaturated fats in the formula. Other tests using only laboratory glassware and chemicals can detect the presence of specific ingredients such as copper phosphates, borax, nitrogen, silicates, rosin, iodine value, saponification, sulfates, chlorides, and wetting agents such as anionic, cationic, or nonionic.

As stated previously, tests on coatings are entirely different from tests on cleaners. We are considering both wax and polymer water-emulsion coatings since these are by far the most commonly used. A polish is developed and tests are designed for the three basic purposes of a coating: to help keep the flooring beautiful, to protect it from wear, and to make it easier to maintain a clean and healthy surface. A liquid coating also has a viscosity, but a thick product is not desirable. Actually, the thinner it is, the better it will spread and level, so the only value of a viscosity test would be to determine fluidity. The Brookfield viscosimeter is the only useful testing device for this property.

Color is important only to make the product as light as possible. If the coating is to be applied on light-colored floors, there should be little or no discoloration. Thus, the discoloration of the dried film on white tile is a more valid test than the color of the liquid. It is possible to make the liquid look light colored and still have the dried film darker.

To check the discoloration on white tile, merely spread equal quantities of the coating onto white panels and allow them to dry. Usually, visual observation is all that is necessary to see differences; however, a reflectometer is convenient for detecting small differences. It utilizes a source of light which is reflected off of the surface onto an electronic eye which transmits the intensity of the reflected light to a numerical scale. Darker surfaces give higher readings.

Odor is checked only for disagreeableness. Very seldom is an odor added merely to give a more pleasing scent. Though the odor of a polish may not be so desirable, it is only a short time before the film dries and the odor disappears. Extremely disagreeable raw materials are avoided in floor polish formulations.

The solids or nonvolatile solids test is equally as important for coverings as for liquid cleaners. It determines the amount of actual polish film contained in the product when applied to floors. The tests are exactly the same. The liquid portion is necessary as a vehicle to give ease of application and to avoid the possibility of streaking. The pH measurement is also the same for cleaners. A mild pH rating is necessary so that there is no harm to the floor surface while the coating is being applied and drying.

Specular gloss shows the ability of a coating film to produce gloss on a surface. A coating is dried on a piece of highly polished black glass, and a gloss meter is used to measure the reflecting power or gloss of this surface. A light source reflects off the surface and an electronic eye transmits it to a numerical scale. In this case the lower-gloss products reduce the original gloss of the black glass, and the highly glossy products do not affect the original gloss of the black glass. An uncoated piece of black glass is always retained for control comparison. Transparency of the film is determined by spreading some of the coating on a piece of glass, or it can be observed on the black glass used for specular gloss. Clearness of the film as compared to the clarity of the glass is recorded. A clear and colorless film brings out the natural beauty of the flooring itself.

A test of the softening point of the solids is run on the solids remaining from evaporating out the volatile material in the oven. The approximate melting point of a buffable wax formula is around 80 degrees C. This test does not apply to the newer polymer formulas because their solids will not melt when heated; they merely char.

Sedimentation or undissolved particles are undesirable in a coating because they may make specks on the floor. The amount of sediment, if any, is found by use of a centrifuge to force the particles to settle to the bottom of a container.

Oven stability tests are important for emulsions as for almost all coatings. An emulsion can be unstable if not properly made, and either separating or jelling may occur. A year is normally considered time enough for a product to be used up by testing in an oven. Heat affects the product in the same way as age. Thus, we have found that one month in an oven at 52 degrees C. is equivalent to one year under normal storage conditions.

Freezing is often harmful to emulsions, so three freeze-and-thaw cycles are always run on wax and polymer formulas. A product may pass one cycle but fail in two. Failure of one of the first three cycles is considered undesirable; however, shipment can be made in heated transportation facilities in the winter for these products. Shipping freezable products can create problems, but not all products can be formulated to pass three freeze cycles. It is sometimes wise to stock up on enough to last through the freezing weather.

Small panels are commonly used for the first series of use tests on floor coatings. Usually, a variety of the most common floor coverings are used. We normally use asphalt, vinyl asbestos, or vinyl and rubber. Linoleum formerly was used, but it is not as commonly encountered in recent years. Two coats are usually applied before tests are begun. Buffable products are buffed between coats. Two products are put on a single panel so they can be compared on an identical surface. Sometimes a standard control product is used on one side.

The first property noticeable in the panel tests is the spreading and leveling ability of the product. Uneven drying and streaking are easily detected. A record is kept of when the coatings appear to be dry. Usually, they dry in only a few minutes. Then the tack-free time is determined by testing with pieces of cotton to see when the coating will be safe for traffic. Usually, it is within one hour. Scuff resistance is checked by rubbing the panel with a fine steel-wool pad. Then the surface is buffed to see how well the marks can be removed. This test applies only to buffable coatings.

The gloss meter is used again on these panels to check the increase in the amount of gloss as determined by comparison with readings taken before the panels were coated. Although a high gloss or shine may seem desirable, many consumers are learning that an average gloss is more easily and economically maintained. The higher the gloss, the quicker marks show up.

Slip tests are run on these panels to eliminate formulas that give slippery films. We use the James slip tester, which is also used by the Underwriters' Laboratories. This machine simulates a situation under which a person falls as naturally as possible, and a chart of the test is recorded. Readings above 0.5 are considered safe while readings below 0.5 are considered slippery. There are numerous other testing devices for checking the slip quality of a floor coating. I can assure you that there are a number of reasons other than the coating itself that can cause a person to fall.

Flexibility and adhesion are tested by simply bending one of the flexible panels and checking for any damaging results. A coating that is too hard and brittle would crumble, and one that does not adhere to the surface would flake off when the panel is bent. This test indicates performance on resilient floors or floors that have some give to them. Dirt retention is found by sprinkling powdered coke on the panel and rolling a heavy, carpeted wheel over it. After brushing off the loose coke, the discoloration is checked as in the discoloration test on white tile.

Water-resisting properties of a coating are checked by two tests. One is the one-hour water-spot test in which a spot of water is left standing on a panel for an hour, blotted off, and allowed to dry. Any effect on the film is recorded. A good water-resisting product will show no effect from this. Small effects are noticeable on many coatings because it is very difficult to obtain a perfectly water-resisting surface and yet one that can easily be removed with water and a little detergent when desired. Much more severe is the two-hour water-immersion test. As the name implies, the panel is immersed in water for two hours, then blotted, and dried. This test should not loosen the film from the panel, but it is difficult to achieve no effect at all from this test.

The abrasive effect of wet traffic on a floor is found by the 25-cycle wet abrasion test. A standard brush is oscillated back and forth for twenty-five cycles over the panel. The brush is wet initially and drops of water are continually added to the surface to maintain a wet condition. After the surface has dried, there should be no noticeable effects of the action.

In a similar fashion a standard cleaning solution is used for seventy-five cycles over a new portion of the tile to test for removability. All the coating should be removed in this test. Thus, the limits of water resistance and removability are defined. A long-term removability test similar to this is sometimes used.

The products that pass the above test satisfactorily are next tested on traffic panels. These panels can be alternated and replaced as desired by the laboratory staff so that close watch can be kept on the results of traffic on them. Once a formula gives good results on these traffic panels, it is then tried on various floors throughout the company, the homes of employees, local stores, or willing customers for the more practical service tests. Just as in cleaner testing, there are numerous analytical tests using the refractometer, gas chromatograph, colorimeter, and other laboratory devices. Raw materials, experimental formulas, and production batches are continually being tested in a busy laboratory.

Thus, you have an idea of the many tests involved for judging the many properties of a product. Nor are these all of them. No one product is ever exceptionally good in all of these properties. Often an improvement in one property reduces the quality of another property. No detergent can claim superior detergency based upon a single property. No floor polish has ever passed all tests without some deficiencies. A good balance of all properties is most desirable in all-purpose products. Claims of a superior finish or cleaner based upon a single property are misleading. Of course, there are specialized products for specific uses only and they should be used for these purposes. I would recommend that you choose a product for the quality and reputation of the company rather than by its price or its appearance on certain approved lists.

Experience in the development and use of chemical products has given me great respect for God and the order of the universe. The chemist has a tremendous task in attempting to duplicate products in nature. Many times man can make a product that in certain respects may be better than the natural product, but he never has completely duplicated this product. Many people look at the tremendous advances that have been gained by chemists and wonder why they now cannot get the perfect product, such as the cleaner that cleans everything without any work involved and the coating that never loses gloss or never wears off. All we can do is bend the natural blend of properties a little more the way we want it, but in so doing we usually develop disadvantages as well. Certainly there will be improvements, but there will always be a need for cleaning and recoating to protect the surface.

DISCUSSION

Question from the floor: I am from the Huntington Library, and while I do not want to deal with the specifics of any brand names at our library, we have been using a plastic finish and have discovered that all during this year the shoes of the employees have been covered with a fine white powder. We wondered if there is any particular explanation for this. It is disastrous because the employees' black shoes come out looking like white bucks.

MR. WILLIAMS: Let us assume that the company from which you bought this product has tested it, and there are two or three of these tests that would detect whether the product was going to powder or would cause powdering, or if the product was too hard and too brittle, or if they used too hard a material and did not plasticize it or did not use a softening agent of the proper formulation. I have seen a few products that would actually powder on any surface.

Let us assume that the company screened the formula and that the product formerly had been a powder and that it even passed some of these tests of powdering or brittleness. If it did pass the tests in the laboratory and would not powder on normal floors, then there is something in the application that causes the powdering. There may be good properties in the product itself, but if the operator does not handle that material properly, then difficulties arise. Now, dusting and powdering can be caused by four or five different sources. The main

one is that if you used a wax previous to applying that polymer coating—you may call it by some other synthetic name—you have a simple adhesion problem. Failure to remove that wax carefully enough usually is the source of the trouble. When you removed the wax and then put another wax on top, you may not have had any trouble. But whenever you remove a wax and put a polymer on top, the polymer just will not stick if all traces of the wax have not been removed.

Waxes are buffable and soft, and they tend to blend in with almost any surface, even old wax or a small trace of wax that was not removed. Whenever you change from wax to polymer, be sure that your custodial help is extra cautious. Once the floor is rid of all of the wax and applications of polymer have begun, then you can start being just a little careless in the removal of it; you can leave a little bit of that polymer on and a new application of polymer will stick to it. A polymer will stick to a polymer, but it will not stick to another wax; the wax will stick to a polymer.

There are other causes of powdering. Perhaps oil was left or spilled on the floor. I have seen cases of powdering in which the coating adhered very well, but there was too much gritty, sandy soil, which is usually the cinder type of soil. In some areas the sand has been weathered and smoothed so that the sand particles are rounded and do not grind as sandpaper does. In other areas where there has been a lot of blasting and disrupting of the natural environment of the ground around the building, usually a new building, then there are sharp edges, pieces of stone and grit or cinder and so on.

Let us review the causes of powdering again. One is the lack of adhesion due to the wax coating still on the floor. The other, if you have removed that wax well and the coating is adhering well, is possible gritty soil. The sharp-edged grit can grind off floor finish.

A polymer coating is hard, and a wax coating is relatively soft. Wax is soft because you want to buff it. You do not have to buff the polymer, but you do stand the chance of scratching it much more. This description fits a few of the properties of these products.

Question from the floor: Would there be any difference in the detergents used for shampooing carpets and those used for cleaning hard coatings on the floor?

MR. WILLIAMS: Yes, you have to consider foam. For instance, you usually need the foam only when working with a carpet, and you never wet a carpet surface as you do another type of floor surface where you just mop it and use the cleaning solution.

In the case of the carpet, you work with the foam. If you have a mechanical apparatus, it works up the foam; if you do not have one, use a very high-foaming product and whip it up yourself in a scrub bucket. To clean the carpet, just use the foam off the top of the bucket. In testing, we dry that film in the oven because we want to see if that film is powdery so that it can be vacuumed away or if it remains as a semiliquid, a paste-like material. The latter is the type of material that redeposits soil easily. The soaps previously used for cleaning all surfaces have certain disadvantages because they leave an oily film. Soap is made of vegetable oil or mineral oil, both of which are liquids, so a layer of liquid is left on that carpet when it is cleaned with soap. But there are detergents that leave a powdery white material which is easily vacuumed away. So you could choose those two particularly, the high-foamy type and the one in which the solids dry, rather than a powdery and a sticky type of foam.

Appendix

Bid Document

The 1966 Equipment Institute focused upon the problems of purchasing library furniture and equipment. Many of those who attended the Institute asked for a typical bid document used in the purchase of library furnishings. The following material has been included in the *Proceedings* in response to those requests.

No two bid documents for library furnishings can be identical; they will vary with local practices and legal requirements, as well as with the experience of the individuals responsible for their preparation. The specifications which follow represent a type which has been used by the compilers in numerous instances and found to be workable and effective. Readers are cautioned, however, that this document cannot be used exactly as presented here, but must be modified to meet the needs of a given situation.

Chapter 3, entitled "Preparation of Bidding Documents . . .," provides a general overview and should be read in conjunction with the use of the following material. Section I (Invitation to Bid), Section II (Instructions to Bidders), and Section III (General Conditions of the Contract) will fit the usual sealed-bid requirements of public and academic libraries. The Bid Proposal Form (pages 85 through 94 of Section II) is one of the most critical sections of the bid document. The format used here has been developed to elicit from bidders all information essential for a proper evaluation of the bids.

Section III, General Conditions of the Contract, consists of a number of standard paragraphs designed to protect and safeguard the purchaser that should always be included in the bid document. However, local legal requirements, the needs of a particular bid situation, and the experience of the individual responsible for preparing the document may indicate the desirability of deleting or adding to the material presented here.

Section IV, the Detailed Specifications and Schedules of Equipment for the several groups of furnishings, serves only to give examples of ways in which this material can be effectively organized. The floor plan (following page 139), included with the bid document, illustrates the manner in which the furniture layout is coded to the specifications.

Washington, D.C.
May 1, 1969

Frazer G. Poole
Robert H. Rohlf

S P E C I F I C A T I O N S for

INTERIOR FURNISHINGS AND EQUIPMENT

for the new

LIBRARY BUILDING

for

_____ (Institution)
_____ (Address)

GRANT PROJECT NO. _____
LOAN PROJECT NO. _____

_____, Business Manager
_____ (Institution)
_____ (Address)

_____, (Date)
Set No. _____

_____ (Architect)
_____ (Address)

_____ (Consultant)
_____ (Address)

TABLE OF CONTENTS

INVITATION TO BID, SECTION I

GRANT PROJECT NO. _____
LOAN PROJECT NO. _____

_____(Institution)
_____(Address)

Separate sealed bids for furnishing and installing Furnishings, Bookstacks,
Draperies, and other Library Equipment, both wood and metal, for the Library
Building presently under construction at _____, will be
received at the Business Office of the _____ until
_____(time), _____(date), and then at said Business
Office publicly opened and read aloud.

The Instructions to Bidders, Specifications, Plans, Bid Proposal forms, form
of Bid Bond, and other information may be examined at the office of _____
_____, Business Manager, at _____. Those wishing to
submit a proposal may secure plans and specifications from said Business
Manager upon payment of a deposit of $25.00 for each set of plans and speci-
fications. Such deposit is refundable upon return of the plans and specifications in good condition, within then (10) days of the opening of bids.

The Owner reserves the right to reject any or all bids, to accept the proposal
of any Bidder for any one Bid Group or any combination of Bid Groups, and to
waive any or all informalities.

No bidder may withdraw his bid within 60 days after actual date of the opening
thereof.

Each bid must be accompanied by cash, certified check of the bidder, or a bid
bond prepared on the form of bid bond attached hereto, duly executed by the
bidder as principal, and having as surety thereon a surety company approved by
the Owner, in the amount of 5% of the bid. Such cash, checks, or bid bonds will
be returned promptly after the Owner and the accepted bidder have executed the
contract, or, if no contract has been awarded within 30 days after the date of
the opening of bids, upon demand of the bidder at any time thereafter, so long
as he has not been notified of the acceptance of his bid.

The successful bidder, upon his failure or refusal to execute and deliver the contract and bonds required within 10 days after he has received notice of the acceptance of his bid, shall forfeit to the Owner, as liquidated damages for such failure or refusal, the security deposited with his bid.

_____ (Institution)

_____ (Address)

_____
        Date

INSTRUCTIONS TO BIDDERS, SECTION II

II-01   RECEIPT AND OPENING OF BIDS:

_____ (hereinafter called the "Owner"), invites bids on the
form attached hereto, all blanks of which must be appropriately filled in. Bids
will be received by the Owner at the Business Office, _____
until 2:00 p.m., C.D.S.T., _____, 1969, and then at said office publicly
opened and read aloud. Envelopes containing the bids must be sealed, addressed
to _____, Business Manager, _____
and identified as bids for INTERIOR FURNISHINGS AND EQUIPMENT, NEW LIBRARY BUILD-
ING, _____.

The Owner may consider informal any bid not prepared and submitted in accordance
with the provisions hereof and may waive any informalities or reject any and all
bids. Any bid may be withdrawn prior to the above scheduled time for the opening of bids or authorized postponement thereof. Any bid received after the time
and date specified will not be considered. No bidder may withdraw his bid for a
period of 60 days after the actual date of the opening thereof.

II-02   PREPARATION OF BIDS:
Pages 85   through 94   of this document, constitute the Bid Proposal form. Three
extra, blank copies of this form for the bidder's use, are provided with each set
of specifications. Each bid must be submitted on the attached Bid Proposal form in
duplicate and certified (signed) by an officer of the bidder's firm with his name
and title indicated. All blank spaces for bid prices, including unit prices, must
be filled in, in ink or with typewriter; both words and figures must be used for
base bids, alternate bids, and lump sum bids. Certification by an appropriate
official of the bidder's firm must be complete and fully executed when submitted.

Each bid must be submitted in a sealed envelope bearing on the outside the name
of the bidder, his address, and the group numbers and names of the furnishings for
which the bid is submitted. If forwarded by mail, the sealed envelope containing the bid must be enclosed in another envelope addressed as specified in the
Bid Proposal form.

II-03   TELEGRAPHIC MODIFICATION:
Any bidder may modify his bid by telegraphic communication at any time prior
to the scheduled closing time for receipt of bids, provided such telegraphic

communication is received by the Owner prior to the closing time, and provided further, the Owner is satisfied that a written confirmation of the telegraphic modification over the signature of the bidder was mailed prior to the closing time. Such telegraphic communication must not reveal the bid price, but should provide only for addition or subtraction or other modification to the original bid, so that final prices or terms will not be known by the Owner until the sealed bid is opened. If written confirmation is not received within two days after the closing time of the bid, no consideration will be given to the telegraphic modification.

II-04   PROCEDURE FOR BIDDING:

The Owner invites bids by individual Groups, by any combination of Groups, or by all Groups combined, as shown below and as set forth in the Detailed Specifications and Schedules of Equipment of Section IV.

Group A - Furnish and install new bookstacks and accessory equipment Items A-1 through A-4, and A-10 through A-43.

Alternate A-1 - Furnish and install new bookstacks and accessory equipment, and disassemble, move, reassemble, and furnish end panels and top bracing for existing stacks, Items A-5 through A-9.

Group B - Furnish and install all technical library furniture, Items B-1 through B-28.

Alternate B-1 - Furnish and install all technical library furniture in Group B, except furnish fifteen (15), 72-tray card catalog cabinets in five (5) units of three (3) each on common leg base.

Group C - Furnish and install office furniture, Items C-1 through C-42C.

Group D - Furnish and install all upholstered seating, Items D-1 through D-3.

Group E - Furnish and install all reading chairs, Items E-1 and E-2.

Group F - Furnish and install all drapery and track in Room Nos. ____, ____, and ____.

II-05   BID PROPOSALS:

The Specifications and Drawings for all work included in this section clearly
set forth the dimensions, sizes, design, sections, gauges, construction methods,
workmanship, etc., and represent a minimum standard of the quality of equipment
desired and on which all Bid Proposals shall be submitted. These requirements
and details shall be complied with exactly in order to obtain the desired results.
Qualified or conditional bids will not be accepted. Only those changes authorized,
in writing, by an Addendum prior to the opening of Bid Proposals will be considered in evaluating the Bid Proposal submitted. Any changes other than these
will be by means of Change Orders after the Award of Contract to the successful
Bidder.

Through testing and other performance requirements, these Specifications require
a desired end result rather than a specific method of manufacture. Wherever,
and whenever in any of the contract documents, an article, material, or equipment
is defined by describing a proprietary product or by using the statement "as
manufactured by", it is the intent of the Owner that this shall describe by reference the material desired, craftsmanship, and method of manufacture, as well as
the size and dimensions rather than to detail all of these requirements herein.
This procedure is not intended to limit bidding to such items, but rather to
establish, by reference to acceptable existing products, a standard of quality
to which the items furnished on this contract must conform.

Every Bidder shall specify, in the appropriate blanks in the Bid Proposal, the
catalog numbers and names or designations of the products he proposes to furnish
in response to these specifications. Where such products are not in accord with
these specifications he shall submit full specifications covering the product he
proposes to furnish.

II-06   WITHDRAWAL OF BIDS:

It is the intent of the **owner** to evaluate and dispose of all bids within 30
days after receipt of bids; however, no bid may be withdrawn for a period of
60 days after the scheduled closing time for receipt of bids.

II-07   BID SECURITY:

Each bid must be accompanied by cash, certified check of the bidder, or a bid
bond prepared on the bid bond form attached hereto, and duly executed by the
bidder as principal, and having as surety thereon a surety company

approved by the Owner, in the amount of 5% of the bid. Such cash, checks, or bid bonds will be returned to all except the three lowest bidders within three days after the opening of bids, and the remaining cash, checks, or bid bonds will be returned promptly after the Owner and the accepted bidder have executed the contract, or, if no award has been made within 30 days after the date of the opening of bids, upon demand of the bidder at any time thereafter, so long as he has not been notified of the acceptance of his bid.

II-08   QUALIFICATIONS OF BIDDERS:

The Owner may make such investigations as he deems necessary to determine the ability of the bidder to perform the work, and the bidder shall furnish to the Owner all such information and data for this purpose as the Owner may request. The Owner reserves the right to reject any bid if the evidence submitted by, or investigations of, such bidder fails to satisfy the Owner that such bidder is properly qualified to carry out the obligations of the contract and to complete the work contemplated therein.

II-09   LIQUIDATED DAMAGES FOR FAILURE TO ENTER INTO CONTRACT:

The successful bidder, upon his failure or refusal to execute and deliver the contract and bonds required within 10 days after he has received the notice of the acceptance of his bid, shall forfeit to the Owner, as liquidated damages for such failure or refusal, the security deposited with his bid.

II-10   DATE OF COMPLETION AND LIQUIDATED DAMAGES:

In his Bid Proposal, the Contractor shall stipulate the number of days required for completion of the contract, for each group of furniture on which he submits a bid. Such statements as "on schedule with the building" are not acceptable and may result in disqualification of the bid. This date, to be stipulated in the contract, is a part of the consideration in awarding this contract, and the Contractor agrees to pay to the Owner, the amount of Fifty Dollars ($50.00), not as a penalty, but as liquidated damages, for each and every calendar day that the Contractor shall be in default after the date stipulated in the contract for completing the Contract.

II-11   ADDENDA AND INTERPRETATIONS:

No interpretation of the meaning of the plans, specifications or other pre-
bid documents will be made to any bidder orally.

Every request for such interpretation should be in writing addressed to

_____, Business Manager, _____,

and to be given consideration must be received at least five days prior to the

date fixed for the opening of bids. Any and all such interpretations, and any

supplemental instructions will be in the form of written addenda to the speci-

fications which, if issued, will be mailed to all prospective bidders (at the

respective addresses furnished for such purposes), not later than three days

prior to the date fixed for the opening of bids. Failure of any bidder to

receive any such addendum or interpretation shall not relieve such bidder from

any obligation under his bid as submitted. All addenda so issued shall become

part of the contract documents.

II-12   APPROVED MANUFACTURERS:

The furnishings for the new library at _____   have been selected

by the owner to harmonize with the design and interior decor of the building and

the names of manufacturers of appropriate and approved designs have been listed

under each group of furnishings. Bidders who wish to bid the products of other

manufacturers shall request permission in writing, indicating the product line

and manufacturer he proposes to furnish, from _____, Business Manager,

_____   not less than ten days prior to the opening of bids. If

such alternate manufacturer is approved, this information will be distributed to

all bidders as a written addendum to the specifications. In the absence of such

approval, the bidder shall bid only in accordance with the original specifications.

II-13   SECURITY FOR FAITHFUL PERFORMANCE:

Simultaneously with his delivery of the executed contract, the Contractor shall

furnish a surety bond or bonds as security for faithful performance of this con-

tract and for the payment of all persons performing labor on the project under

this contract and furnishing materials in connection with this contract, as

specified in the General Conditions included herein. The surety on such bond

or bonds shall be a duly authorized surety company satisfactory to the Owner.

II-14   SAMPLES:

After bids have been opened, the owner may, at his discretion, request samples in

order to arrive at a determination in the award of the contract. Such samples

II-14   <u>SAMPLES CONTINUED</u>:

must be delivered within ten (10) days after notification by the owner. No
samples will be required prior to the receipt of bids.

II-15   <u>TESTS</u>:

Appropriate tests for finishes and general performance have been included in
these specifications. The owner reserves the right to have such tests conducted
by a qualified testing laboratory at any time after delivery of the furnishings
begins, and to require that products submitted by bidders do, in fact, conform
to the requirements of these specifications. Or the owner may require a certification of such performance from the manufacturer as a condition for the award
of the contract.

BID PROPOSAL FORM[1]   Page 1

                                        Place:

                                        Date:

To:

     Mr. _____

     Business Manager

     _____ (Institution)

     _____ (Address)

Proposal for:

     Interior Furnishings and Equipment for the new

     Library Building

     _____ (Institution)

     _____ (Address)

Submitted by:

     Firm Name: _____

     Address: _____

     Telephone No.: _____

Gentlemen:

The above named Bidder, a corporation organized and existing under the
laws of the State of _____, a partnership, an individual,[2]
in compliance with your invitation for bids for furnishing and installing
various interior furnishings and equipment, both wood and metal, in the new
library building presently under construction at _____ having familiar-
ized himself with the local conditions, and having examined the specifications
and the plans, hereby proposes to **furnish,** set in place, and install all

---

[1]Three blank copies of this form (pages 85 through 94) are inserted at the
back of these specifications. Your bid is to be submitted in duplicate on
this form. The third copy should be retained for your files.

[2]Cross out inapplicable terms.

furnishings and to provide all labor, materials, and transportation necessary to complete such work at the prices set forth below.

The Bidder further agrees to commence work as soon as the contract has been awarded, and hereby certifies that the work will be completed within the number of days from the signing of the contract which is stipulated in this Bid Proposal. The Bidder further agrees to pay as liquidated damages, not as a penalty, the sum of Fifty Dollars ($50.00) for each consecutive calendar day, in excess of the number of days stipulated, during which the work remains incomplete.

The Bidder acknowledges receipt of the following addenda:

_____

_____

_____

_____

_____

BASE BID PROPOSALS AND ALTERNATES UNDER GROUPS A, B, C, D, E, AND F

(NOTE TO BIDDER: In the following proposal the amount of the total bid for all groups shall be shown in both words and figures. In case of a discrepancy between the two, the amount in words shall govern.)

BASE BID PROPOSAL GROUP A - STEEL BOOKSTACKS:

Bidder agrees to furnish and install all new bookstacks and accessory equipment specified and described in the Detailed Specifications and/or listed in the Schedule of Equipment and shown on the drawings, Sheet Nos. 1-3, items A-1 through A-4, and items A-10 through A-43, for the total sum of: _____

_____ Dollars ($_____).

Bidder proposes to furnish new bookstacks as manufactured by _____ whose manufacturing plant is located in _____, and whose home office is at _____.

GROUP A - STEEL BOOKSTACKS; ALTERNATE NO. A-1:

Bidder agrees to furnish and install all new bookstacks and accessory equipment specified and described in the Base Bid Proposal for Group A, and to disassemble, move, and reassemble in locations indicated on the drawings, Sheet No. 1, and to furnish end panels and top bracing for those bookstacks now owned by _____ College and listed in the Schedule of Equipment and shown on the drawings as items A-5 through A-9, for the additional sum of: _____

_____Dollars ($_____).

BASE BID PROPOSAL   GROUP B - TECHNICAL LIBRARY FURNITURE:

Bidder agrees to furnish and install all technical library furniture as specified and described in the Detailed Specifications and/or as listed in the Schedule of Equipment and shown on the drawings, Sheet Nos. 1-3, items B-1 through B-28, for the sum of: _____

_____Dollars ($_____).

Bidder proposes to furnish technical library furniture as manufactured by _____, whose manufacturing plant is located in _____, and whose home office is at _____.

Library furniture to be supplied by this bidder is designated as the manufacturer's _____[1] line.

GROUP B - TECHNICAL LIBRARY FURNITURE, ALTERNATE NO. B-1:

Bidder agrees to furnish and install all technical library furniture as specified and described in the Detailed Specifications and/or as listed in the Schedule of Equipment and shown on the drawings, items B-1 through B-28, except Item B-8 to be furnished in units of three, 72-tray card catalog cabinets each on a common, steel frame leg base (5 groups of three, 72-tray cabinets), for the sum of: _____

_____Dollars ($_____).

---

[1]This information must be supplied if applicable.

BASE BID PROPOSAL GROUP B - TECHNICAL LIBRARY FURNITURE, UNIT PRICES:

Item No.	Catalog No.	Description	Unit Price	Quantity	Total Price
B-1		Reading Table, 72"x42"		7	
B-2		Study Carrels, 36"x24"		103	
B-3		Reading Tables, 72"x48"		13	
B-4		Dictionary Stand		6	
B-5		Card Catalog Cabinet, 30-tray		1	
B-6		Record Browsing Tub		1	
B-7		Cumulative Book Index Table		1	
B-8		Card Catalog Cabinet, separate steel frame leg bases, each cabinet with top, sides, and back		15	
B-8		Card Catalog Cabinet, three 72-tray units on common leg base (Alternate No. B-1)		5	
B-9		Depressible Book Trucks		2	
B-10		Slipping Truck		1	
B-11		Catalog Reference Table, 60"x24"		4	
B-12		Reading Table, 60"x42"		4	
B-13		Study Carrels, 4 double units in tandem (7 groups of 8 each)		56 study units	
B-13a		As above, except 5 double units in tandem (1 group of 10 units)		10 study units	
B-14		Index Table, 72"x48"		3	
B-15		Map Case		1	
B-16		Atlas Case		1	
B-17		Bibliography shelves		5 (4'units)	

GROUP B - TECHNICAL LIBRARY FURNITURE, UNIT PRICES CONTINUED:

Item No.	Catalog No.	Description	Unit Price	Quantity	Total Price
B-18		Exhibit Case, table type 84"x27"		1	
B-19		Exhibit Case, upright, movable		1	
B-20		Card Catalog Cabinet, 4-drawer unit		6	
B-21		Card Catalog Cabinet, 4-drawer unit		1	
B-22		Dictionary Stand, revolving		2	
B-23		Reading Table, 60"x36"		2	
B-24		Bookcases, special for Rare Book room, 36"x15" deep x 84" high		11	
B-25		Table, special, 61"x39"		1	
B-26		Bookcases, special, 73"x62" high (new book shelves)		2	
B-27		Step Stools		20	

BASE BID PROPOSAL GROUP C - STEEL OFFICE FURNITURE:

Bidder agrees to furnish and install all office furniture specified and described in the Detailed Specifications and/or listed in the Schedule of Equipment and shown on the drawings, Sheet Nos. 1-3, Items C-1 through C-42B, for the sum of: _____

_____ Dollars ($_____).

Bidder proposes to furnish steel office furniture as manufactured by _____

_____, whose manufacturing plant is located in _____,

and whose home office is at _____.

Steel office furniture to be supplied by this bidder is designated as the manufacturer's _____[1] line.

BASE BID PROPOSAL GROUP C - STEEL OFFICE FURNITURE, UNIT PRICES:

Item No.	Catalog No.	Description	Unit Price	Quantity	Total Price
C-1		Desk, double pedestal w/TU		5	

[1]This information must be supplied if applicable.

BASE BID PROPOSAL GROUP C - STEEL OFFICE FURNITURE, UNIT PRICES CONTINUED:

Item No.	Catalog No.	Description	Unit Price	Quantity	Total Price
C-2		Desk, double pedestal w/TU		5	
C-3		Swivel Chair		13	
C-4		Side Chair		11	
C-5		Lateral Files		8	
C-6		Bookcases		3	
C-7		Add-on Unit (storage)		6	
C-8		Posture Chairs		33	
C-9		Desk, double pedestal		10	
C-10		Storage Cabinets		12	
C-11		Storage Cabinets		2	
C-12		Legal Files, 4-drawer		14	
C-13		Letter Files, 4-drawer		14	
C-14		Desk, double pedestal w/TU		12	
C-15		Legal Files, 5-drawer		8	
C-16		Table, 70"x36"		2	
C-17		Table, typing		1	
C-18		Desk, single pedestal w/TU		1	
C-19		Table, 60"x30"		1	
C-20		Desk, single pedestal w/TU		3	
C-21		Desk, single pedestal w/TU		1	
C-22		Letter File, 2-drawer		1	
C-23		Legal File, 5-drawer		10	
C-24		Stacking Chairs		126	
C-24a		Stacking Chair Dolly		6	
C-25		Microfilm Storage Files		9	
C-26		Microcard Storage Files		1	
C-27		Table, conference, 84"x36"		4	
C-28		Table, conference, 48"x36"		1	
C-29		Table, conference, 96"x42"		1	
C-30		Table, conference, 180"x48"		1	
C-31		Table, conference, 96"x42"		1	
C-32		Table, occasional, 45"x19"		3	
C-33		Table, occasional, 30"x30"		13	

BASE BID PROPOSAL GROUP C - STEEL OFFICE FURNITURE, UNIT PRICES CONTINUED:

Item No.	Catalog No.	Description	Unit Price	Quantity	Total Price
C-34		Table, occasional, 42"diam.		4	
C-35		Table, occasional, 42"diam.		1	
C-36		Side Chair, w/arms		12	
C-37		Side Chair, w/o arms		52	
C-38		Swivel Chair, w/arms		5	
C-39		Swivel Chair, w/arms		1	
C-40 & 40a		Steel Office Partitions		10 (3'-panels)	
C-41		Wastebaskets w/satin chrome legs		16	
C-42		Letter Trays, legal size		16	
C-42a		Letter Trays, letter size		16	
C-42b		Stacking plates for above letter trays		16	

BASE BID PROPOSAL GROUP D - UPHOLSTERED SEATING:

Bidder agrees to furnish and install all upholstered furniture specified and described in the Detailed Specifications and/or listed in the Schedule of Equipment and shown on the drawings, Sheet Nos. 1-3, Items D-1 through D-3, for the sum of: _____

_____ Dollars ($_____).

Bidder proposes to furnish upholstered seating as manufactured by _____, whose manufacturing plant is located in _____ and whose home office is at _____. Upholstery fabrics will be _____ 100% nylon, Scotchgard treated.

BASE BID PROPOSAL GROUP D - UPHOLSTERED SEATING, UNIT PRICES:

Item No.	Catalog No.	Description	Unit Price	Quantity	Total Price
D-1		Settee, 2-seater, _____ 100% nylon, Scotchgard treated fabric		3	
D-2		Settee, 3-seater, _____ 100% nylon, Scotchgard-treated fabric		6	
D-2		Settee, 3-seater, _____ expanded vinyl.		1	

BASE BID PROPOSAL GROUP D - UPHOLSTERED SEATING, UNIT PRICES CONTINUED:

Item No.	Catalog No.	Description	Unit Price	Quantity	Total Price
D-2		Settee, 3-seater, _____ 100% nylon fabric, tufted upholstery		5	
D-3		Club chair, _____ 100% nylon fabric, plain upholstery		67	

BASE BID PROPOSAL GROUP E - READING CHAIRS:

Bidder agrees to furnish and install all reading chairs as specified or described in the Detailed Specifications and/or as listed in the Schedule of Equipment and shown on the drawings, Items E-1 and E-2, in _____ Scotchgard-treated, 100% nylon fabric, for the sum of: _____ _____ Dollars ($ _____).

Bidder proposes to furnish reading chairs as manufactured by _____, whose manufacturing plant is located in _____, and whose home office is at _____. Reading chairs to be supplied by this bidder are designated as the manufacturer's _____[1] line.

BASE BID PROPOSAL GROUP E - READING CHAIRS, UNIT PRICES:

Item No.	Catalog No.	Description	Unit Price	Quantity	Total Price
E-1		Reading chair, w/o arms, in 100% nylon fabric		96	
E-2		Reading chair, w/arms, in 100% nylon fabric		193	

---

[1]This information must be supplied if applicable.

Group E - Reading Chairs, Alternate No. E-1, Unit prices:

Item No.	Catalog No.	Description	Unit Price	Quantity	Total Price
E-1		Reading Chair, w/o arms, _____ 100% nylon, Scotchgard-treated fabric		96	
E-2		Reading Chair, w/arms, _____ 100% nylon, Scotchgard-treated fabric		193	

BASE BID PROPOSAL   GROUP F - DRAPERIES:

Bidder agrees to furnish all materials, hardware, and incidentals, and to fabricate, install, and adjust all draperies, as specified and described in the Detailed Specifications and as listed in the Draperies Schedule and shown on the plans, in Rooms Nos. ___, ___, ____, and ____, for the sum of:

_____ (Dollars ($_____).

COMBINED BID

(NOTE TO BIDDER: In making a combined bid of two or more groups, bidder shall indicate group numbers and names of all groups he proposes to furnish under this procedure.)

Bidder agrees to furnish and install Groups _____

_____,

as described in the Detailed Specifications, listed in the Schedule of Equipment, and indicated on the drawings for the sum of: _____

_____ Dollars ($_____).

We understand that time is of the essence in the fulfillment of this Contract and we submit the following as our best delivery schedule (in calendar days from date contract is signed) for:

> Group A _____ calendar days
>
> Group B _____ calendar days
>
> Group C _____ calendar days

Group D _____ calendar days

Group E _____ calendar days

Group F _____ calendar days

In accordance with the requirements of the specifications, the undersigned has attached[1] to this <u>Bid Proposal</u> form a certificate of guarantee[2] from the manufacturer(s) of the furnishings we propose to supply, as follows:

____ Group A - Steel Bookstacks: five (5) years

____ Group B - Technical Library Furniture: three (3) years

____ Group C - Steel Office Furniture: three(3) years

____ Group D - Upholstered Seating: frame: (5) years; upholstery: two (2) years

____ Group E - Reading Chairs: three (3) years

____ Group F - Draperies: two (2) years

Bidder understands that the Owner reserves the right to reject any or all bids and to waive any informalities in the bidding.

The bidder agrees this bid shall be good and may not be withdrawn for a period of 60 calendar days after the scheduled closing time for receiving bids.

Upon receipt of written notice of the acceptance of this bid, the Bidder will execute the formal contract within 10 days and deliver Surety Bond to the Owner. The bid security attached in the sum of _____ Dollars ($_____) is to become the property of the Owner in the event contract and bond are not executed within the time set forth, as liquidated damages for the delay and additional expense to the Owner caused thereby.

Respectfully submitted,

By _____

Title _____

Business Address

SEAL
(If bid is by a corporation)

_____

[1]Indicate guarantees attached by checking appropriate box(s).
[2]Failure to attach manufacturer's guarantee may result in rejection of bid as non-responsive.

:FORM FOR BID BOND

<u>BID BOND</u>

KNOW ALL MEN BY THESE PRESENTS, that we, the undersigned, _____

_____as Principal, and

_____as Surety, are hereby held

and firmly bound unto _____as owner

in the penal sum of _____

for the payment of which, well and truly to be made, we hereby jointly and

severally bind ourselves, our heirs, executors, administrators, successors

and assigns.

Signed, this _____ day of _____, 19__.

The condition of the above obligation is such that whereas the Principal has

submitted to _____ a certain Bid,

attached hereto and hereby made a part hereof to enter into a contract in

writing, for the _____

_____

_____

_____

NOW, THEREFOR,

a) If said Bid shall be rejected, or in the alternate,

b) If said Bid shall be accepted and the Principal shall execute and deliver
a contract in the Form of Contract attached hereto (properly completed in
accordance with said Bid) and shall furnish a bond for his faithful performance
of said contract, and for the payment of all persons performing labor or
furnishing materials in connection therewith, and shall in all other respects
perform the agreement created by the acceptance of said Bid,

then this obligation shall be void, otherwise the same shall remain in force
and effect; it being expressly understood and agreed that the liability of

the Surety for any and all claims hereunder shall, in no event, exceed the penal amount of this obligation as herein stated.

The Surety, for value received, hereby stipulates and agrees that the obligations of said Surety and its bond shall be in no way impaired or affected by any extension of the time within which the Owner may accept such Bid; and said Surety does hereby waive notice of any such extension.

IN WITNESS WHEREOF, the Principal and the Surety have hereunto set their hands and seals, and such of them as are corporations have caused their corporate seals to be hereto affixed and these presents to be signed by their proper officers, the day and year first set forth above.

_____(L.S.)
                    Principal

_____
                    Surety

SEAL   By:_____

GENERAL CONDITIONS OF THE CONTRACT, SECTION III

III-01   DEFINITIONS:

a) The following definitions apply to this contract:

OWNER . . . . Owner, within meaning of contract documents, is _____.
The Owner may act through any duly authorized representative thereof.

BUSINESS MANAGER . . . . . ._____

_____

ARCHITECT . . . . _____

_____

CONSULTANT . . . . _____

_____

APPROVED . . . . Terms such as "as approved by" or similar words or phrases are to be understood to mean action on the part of the Owner or his duly authorized representatives, the Architect and/or Consultant.

III-02   INSPECTION:

a) All materials furnished and work done will be inspected by the Owner and if not in accordance with these specifications, will be rejected and shall be immediately removed, and other materials furnished and work done in accordance therewith.

b) If the Contractor refuses to remove the work and material as above, when ordered to do so, then the Owner shall have the right and authority to stop the Contractor and his work at once, and to supply men and materials to remove and correct the faulty work and materials at the cost and expense of the Contractor. Such expense is to be deducted from any money then due or to become due the Contractor from the Owner.

c) If, however, the Owner shall fail or neglect to correct any faulty or defective materials or work, as outlined above, the Contractor shall not be relieved of correcting said materials or work, and the right of final acceptance or condemnation of the work shall not be waived in any manner by reason of said failure or neglect on the part of the Owner.

d) The Health, Education and Welfare Administrator, and his authorized representatives and agents or any other representative of the Government shall be permitted to inspect all furniture and/or equipment, materials, pay rolls, records of personnel, invoices of materials and other relevant data and records.

III-03   ASSIGNMENTS:

The Contractor shall not assign the whole or any part of this contract or any moneys due or to become due hereunder without written consent of the Owner. In case the Contractor assigns all or any part of any moneys due or to become due under this contract, the instrument of assignment shall contain a clause substantially to the effect that it is agreed that the right of the assignee in and to any moneys due or to become due to the Contractor shall be subject to prior liens of all persons, firms, and corporations for services rendered or materials supplied for the performance of the work called for in this contract.

III-04   TIME AND ORDER OF COMPLETION AND LIQUIDATED DAMAGES:

a) The work shall be commenced and carried on at such point and in such order of precedence and at such times and seasons as the Architect directs. Owner reserves the right to entirely discontinue said work, should the condition of the weather make it desirable to do so, and in order that the work may be well and properly executed.

b) When the Contractor is delayed so that completion within the time specified is unlikely, he may apply for an extension of time, in writing, within ten (10) days after a delay occurs. The request shall state the cause of the delay and the extension requested. Owner will review the request and grant, deny, or adjust the request on its merits.

c) Contractor agrees that he will sustain all losses or damages arising from the action of the elements, the nature of the work or from any casualty. Should the Owner be prevented or enjoined from authorizing its prosecution, either before or after commencement, by reason of any litigation or by reason of its inability to procure any lands or rights of way for the said work, Contractor shall not be entitled to make or assert claim for damage by reason of said delay, nor withdraw from the contract except by consent of the Owner. Time for completion of the work shall be extended for such time as Owner determines will compensate for the time lost by such delay, with such determination to be set forth in writing.

d) In his Proposal, the Contractor shall stipulate the number of days required for ^completion of the contract, for each group of furniture on which he submits a bid. It is hereby understood and mutually agreed to, by and between the parties hereto, that the time within which the furniture and/or equipment hereunder are to be furnished, delivered, and installed in the Library is an ESSENTIAL CONDITION of this Contract. IF THE SAID CONTRACTOR SHALL NEGLECT, FAIL, OR REFUSE TO FURNISH, DELIVER, AND INSTALL THE FURNITURE AND/OR EQUIPMENT WITHIN THE TIME LIMITS STIPULATED IN THE CONTRACT, (as stipulated in his Proposal), then said Contractor shall agree, as a part of the consideration for the awarding of this Contract, to pay to the Owner the amount of Fifty Dollars ($50.00), not as a penalty, but as liquidated damages for each and every calendar day that the Contractor shall be in default after the date stipulated in the Contract for completing the Contract. The said amount is fixed and agreed upon by and between the Contractor and the Owner because of the impracticability and extreme difficulty of fixing and ascertaining the actual damages the Owner would in such event sustain, and said amount is agreed to be the amount of damages which the Owner would sustain and said amounts shall be retained by the Owner from the payment due the Contractor.

e) Provided, that the Contractor shall not be charged with liquidated damages or any excess cost when the delay in completion of the work is due:

    1) To any preference, priority, or allocation order duly issued by the Government; or

    2) To unforseeable cause beyond the control and without the fault or negligence of the Contractor, including, but not restricted to, acts of God or of the public enemy, acts of the Owner, fires, floods, epidemics, quarantine restrictions, strikes and freight embargoes.

f) Provided, further, that the Contractor shall, within seven (7) days from the beginning of such delay, notify the Owner, in writing, of the causes of the delay, who shall ascertain the facts and extent of the delay and notify the Contractor within a reasonable time of its decision in the matter.

III-05 MATERIALS AND LABOR:
a) The Contractor is to furnish, at his own cost and expense, all of the labor, materials, tools, expendable equipment, and utility and transportation services required to perform and complete the work in the best possible and most expeditious manner according to the drawings and specifications.

b) He shall employ only competent foremen and experienced laborers, and shall discharge immediately, whenever required to do so by the Architect, any man considered by the Architect to be incompetent or disposed to be disorderly. He shall not again employ such person on this work.

c) The Contractor shall acquire materials locally, where practicable, and shall employ local labor, including skills and supervision, if available.

d) The Contractor agrees to pay all claims for labor performed and materials furnished in completing the contract.

III-06   PERMITS AND REGULATIONS:

The Contractor shall procure and pay for all permits, licenses, and approvals necessary for the execution of his contract. He shall comply with all laws, ordinances, rules, orders, and regulations relating to the performance of the work, the protection of adjacent property and the maintenance of passageways, guard fences or other protective facilities. He shall follow, without delay, all instructions and orders given by the Architect in the performance of his work.

III-07   COOPERATION WITH OTHER CONTRACTORS:

The Contractor is required, so far as is possible, to arrange his work and to dispose of his materials as not to interfere with the work or storage of materials of other contractors engaged upon the work.

III-08   CLAIMS:

a) Before the final settlement will be made, the Contractor must furnish to the Owner satisfactory evidence that all persons who have been employed upon the work, or who have furnished materials for the work under his contract and according to these specifications, and may have been entitled to a lien, have been fully settled with and are no longer entitled to a lien.

b) In case such evidence is not furnished, then the Owner may retain from all monies due to the Contractor, and in possession of the Owner, such an amount as they may deem necessary to meet all lawful claims due to the above-mentioned parties until such claims are fully discharged, and theevidence thereof furnished to the Owner.

III-09   MEASUREMENTS:

The work included in this contract shall be carefully fitted in place. The Contractor shall verify all measurements at the building, and shall be responsible for the correctness of same where the fitting of his work is affected.

III-10   INSTALLATION:

a) Installation shall be done under supervision of authorized agent of the Contractor.

b) Set all items in place as shown on Drawings.

c) Set with tops level.

d) Clean, oil or polish as required.

e) Remove all crating and debris from project.

f) Leave premises in showroom condition, all items free from dust.

g) Installation shall be over carpeting. Contractor shall make all provisions necessary, and shall take special precautions to protect carpet.

III-11   PROTECTION:

a) Protect the building, as necessary, to prevent damage.

b) Any work damaged shall be restored to original condition, and Contractor shall be charged with the expense thereof.

III-12   STORAGE:

a) No provision for temporary storage has been made.

b) The Contractor shall make provision and pay for storage space until such time as building is ready for installation.

III-13   DELIVERY:

All deliveries shall be coordinated with the Architect and General Contractor.

III-14   TAXES:

a) Materials and equipment incorporated into this project are exempt from the payment of Sales Tax under the laws of the State of Iowa,   and such tax shall not be included in the proposal of the bidders.

b) The Owner shall provide the Contractor with a proper exemption certificate within ten (10) days of the contract date. Should the Owner fail to provide an exemption certificate within the required time period, the Contractor shall notify the Architect in writing. In the event that the Owner elects to proceed on a non-exempt basis, the contract amount shall be equitably adjusted, in writing, in a lump sum amount sufficient to cover the Contractor's sales tax expense.

c) Upon issuance of a proper exemption certificate to the Contractor, the
Contractor shall assume full responsibility for his own proper use of the certificate, and shall pay all costs of any legally-assessed penalties relating to
the Contractor's improper use of the exemption certificate.

III-15   EXTRA CHARGES:

The bid price shall be for complete installation, ready for Owner's use, and
shall include all applicable freight charges and all installation charges. No
extra charges will be allowed.

III-16   SHOP DRAWINGS:

a) The Contractor must submit a reproducible transparency of each drawing, for
the Architect's approval, where called for in the specifications.

b) Approval of shop drawings by the Architect will be general. It shall not
relieve the Contractor of the responsibility for the accuracy of such shop drawings, nor for proper fitting, construction of work, furnishing of materials or
work required by contract and not indicated on the shop drawings. Shop drawing
approval shall not be construed as approving departures from contract documents.

III-17   LABELS:

There shall be no labels or manufacturers' or suppliers' identification on any
exposed portions of any furniture or equipment. Failure to comply will be cause
for rejection.

III-18   WAGE RATES:

There shall be paid each laborer or mechanic or the Contractor or Subcontractors
engaged in work on the project under this contract not less than the hourly wage
rate established by the United States Secretary of Labor, regardless of any con-
tractual relationship which may be alleged to exist between the Contractor or
any Subcontractor and such laborers and mechanics.

III-19   "OR EQUAL" CLAUSE:

Where any article or thing in these documents is specified by a proprietary name,
a trade name, or the name of a manufacturer, with the addition of the expression
"or approved equal," it is understood: (1) that the Consultant, acting as the
Owner's representative, will use his own judgment in determining whether or not
any article proposed as an alternate is the equal of any article specified
herein; (2) that the decision of the Consultant on all such questions of equality

shall be final; and (3) that in the event of any adverse decision by the
Consultant, acting as the Owner's representative, no claim of any sort
shall be made or allowed against the Consultant or the Owner by the manufacturer, jobber, or other supplier of the articles involved.

III-20   DAMAGES AND PATENTS:

a) The Contractor will be required by his contract to save the Owner and
its officers, agents, and employees harmless from liability of any nature
or kind whatever, in connection with his work or any part thereof, during
the manufacture, delivery, and installation of all furnishings and equipment
until the same has been accepted by the Owner. He shall pay all losses,
damages, or claims that the Owner may be liable for, and shall save the
Owner harmless in all things, from any accident or casualty, damages,
losses, or claims which may happen or arise by any failure, neglect, or
refusal on his part or that of his agents to prevent the same.

b) If the Contractor uses any design, device, or materials covered by
letters patent or copyright, he shall provide for such use by suitable
agreement with the Owner of such patented or copyrighted device or material.
It is mutually agreed and understood, without exception, that the contract
price shall include all royalties or costs arising from the use of such
design, device or materials, in any way involved in the work. The Contractor and/or his sureties shall indemnify and save harmless the Owner from
any and all claims for infringement by reason of the use of such patented
or copyrighted design, device, or materials, or any trademark or copyright
in connection with work agreed to be performed under this contract, and
shall indemnify the Owner for any cost, expense, or damage it may be obliged
to pay by reason of such infringement at any time during the prosecution
of the work or after completion of the work.

c) License or Royalty Fees: License and/or Royalty Fees for the use of
a process which is authorized by the Owner must be reasonable, and paid to
the holder of patent, or his authorized licensee, direct by the Owner, and
not by or through the Contractor.

III-21   PAYMENTS:

a) On the first day of the month following delivery of items of furniture and/or equipment and/or bookstacks to the building, the Contractor may submit to the Business Manager of the College application for payment for such items; and the Owner will, within ten days of receipt of such request, pay to the Contractor ninety (90%) percent of such amount; and within thirty (30) days after completion of all requirements of the Contract, the Owner will pay the Contractor the balance of the total contract sum.

b) The Contractor shall submit to the Business Manager of the College an application for each payment, on or before the first day of the month; and if required, shall provide receipts or other vouchers, in evidence of his payment for materials and labor including payments to manufacturers, jobbers, subcontractors and other suppliers.

c) In applying for payments, the Contractor shall submit a statement based upon items delivered and set in place on the Owner's premises, and if required, itemized in such form and supported by such additional evidence as the Business Manager may direct, showing his right to the payment claimed.

d) Payments will be made on account of items and materials delivered and suitably stored on the premises but not finally assembled, but they shall, if required by the Business Manager, be conditional upon submission by the Contractor of evidence of value of such items and materials, and bills of sale or such other procedure as will establish the Owner's title of such material or otherwise adequately protect the Owner's interest.

III-22   INSURANCE:

The Contractor shall not commence work under this contract until he has obtained all the insurance required under this paragraph and such insurance has been approved by the Owner, nor shall the Contractor allow any subcontractor to commence work on his subcontract until the insurance requirements of the subcontractor have been so obtained and approved.

a) Compensation Insurance. The Contractor shall procure and shall maintain during the life of this contract Workmen's Compensation Insurance as required by applicable State or territorial laws for all of his employees to be engaged in work at the site of the project under this contract, and in case of any such work sublet, the Contractor shall require the subcontractor similarly to provide Workmen's Compensation Insurance for all of the latter's employees, to be engaged in such work unless such employees are covered by the protection

afforded by the Contractor's Workmen's Compensation Insurance. In case any
class of employees engaged in hazardous work on the project under this contract
is not protected under the Workmen's Compensation Statute, the Contractor shall
provide and shall cause each subcontractor to provide adequate employer's
liability insurance for the protection of such of his employees as are not otherwise protected.

b) Contractor's Public Liability and Property Damage Insurance and Vehicle
Liability Insurance. The Contractor shall procure and shall maintain during
the life of this contract Contractor's Public Liability Insurance, Contractor's
Property Damage Insurance and Vehicle Liability Insurance in the following
amounts: Each Contractor's Public Liability Insurance and Vehicle Liability
Insurance shall be in an amount not less than $250,000 for injuries, including
accidental death, to any one person, and subject to the same limit for each person, in an amount not less than $500,000 on account of one accident, and Contrac-
tor's Property Damage Insurance in an amount not less than $100,000.

c) Subcontractor's Public Liability and Property Damage Insurance and Vehicle
Liability Insurance. The Contractor shall either 1) require each of his subcontractors to procure and to maintain during the life of his subcontract, the
Subcontractor's Public Liability and Property Damage Insurance and Vehicle
Liability Insurance of the type and in amounts specified above, or shall 2)
insure the activities of his subcontractors in his own policy, as specified
above.

d) Scope of Insurance and Special Hazards: The insurance required under sub-
paragraphs b) and c) hereof shall provide adequate protection for the Contractor
and his subcontractors respectively, against damage claims which may arise from
operations under this contract whether such operations be by the insured or by
anyone directly or indirectly employed by him.

e) Proof of Carriage of Insurance: The Contractor shall furnish the Owner
with certificates showing the type, amount, class of operations covered, effective dates and date of expiration of policies. The insurance covered by this
certificate will not be cancelled or materially altered, except after ten (10)
days written notice has been received by the Owner.

III-24   ACCEPTANCE AND GUARANTEE:
a) A formal inspection of the work will be made by the Owner within thirty

(30) days after the completion of same. At that time, should any defects or imperfections appear in the whole or any part of the work, caused by or due to any fault or negligence of the contractor, the same must be corrected before the work will be accepted. Otherwise, the work will be accepted at that time.

b) Neither the final certificate of payment or any provision in the contract documents nor partial or entire use of the furniture, equipment and/or supplies by the Owner shall constitute an acceptance thereof if not in accordance with Contract Documents or relieve the Contractor of liability in respect to any express warranties or responsibility for faulty materials or workmanship. The Contractor shall promptly remedy any defects without cost to the Owner, which appear within a period of one year from the date of final acceptance unless a longer period is specified. The Owner will give notice of observed defects with reasonable promptness.

III-25   PLANS:

The plans listed below are part of these specifications and all bidders must be familiar with them. Code numbers on the plans correspond with those listed in the Schedules of Equipment. Plans included in these specifications consist of:

> Sheet No. 1   Lower Floor Plan
> Sheet No. 2   Main Floor Plan
> Sheet No. 3   Upper Floor Plan
> Sheet No. 4   Details of Special Items of Furniture

DETAILED SPECIFICATIONS AND SCHEDULES OF EQUIPMENT

SECTION IV

GROUP A - STEEL BOOKSTACKS
DETAILED SPECIFICATIONS

IV-A-01   GENERAL

a) All applicable provisions of the General Conditions, Section III, govern
work under this Group.

b) These specifications contemplate the installation of equipment of the
highest type as measured by the standards of the bookstack industry. First
quality workmanship and materials will be required throughout. Items referred
to and required in the specifications but not called for on the drawings, or
items shown on the drawings and coded to the Schedule of Equipment for this
Group, but not actually referred to in the specifications, shall be furnished
as if fully covered by both drawings and specifications. Items are properly
identified on the equipment drawings and it shall be the bidder's responsibility
to properly count and/or list and to be responsible for furnishing all items
required.

IV-A-02 SCOPE

a) The work required under this heading includes all labor, materials, appli-
ances, tools, and equipment, and the performance of all operations necessary
for the complete execution and installation of bookstacks as shown, detailed,
and/or scheduled in the drawings: Sheets 1 through 3, and/or _____ in the
specifications under Group A - Steel Bookstacks and itemized under the
Schedule of Equipment.

b) Bookstacks designated A-5 through A-9 (shaded on the drawings), located
on the lower floor, will be furnished by Owner from existing equipment. These
stacks were originally supplied by _____. Alternate No. 1, Group A
requires the disassembly of these stacks in the old library and their reassembly
in the new library in the locations shown on the drawing. The contractor is to
visit the site and inspect these stacks. No refinishing is required.

c) No end panels are installed on the existing stacks and this contract
requires that end panels be provided and installed. (See Alternate No. 1.)

GROUP A - STEEL BOOKSTACKS
DETAILED SPECIFICATIONS

IV-A-03   <u>APPROVED MANUFACTURERS</u>:

The following manufacturers only are approved for bidding on GROUP A, Steel Bookstacks:

a)

b)

c)

d)

e)

GROUP A - STEEL BOOKSTACKS
DETAILED SPECIFICATIONS

IV-A-04 MATERIALS

Materials used in fulfilling the requirements of these specifications shall
be the best of their respective kind and those best adapted to the construction
for which they are to be employed and shall meet these following General
Specifications:

a) Cold-rolled structural members - heavy gauge materials, from eleven gauge
through eighteen gauge in thickness, shall be of at least grade C steel con-
forming to the requirements of A.S.T.M. A245-T Grade C.

b) Sheet steel forming the various parts of the work, shall be made of the
best grade of sheet steel known as "Metallic Furniture" stock, American,
open-hearth, cold-rolled, reannealed, whole pickled and free from scale and
buckle. All gauges shall be U.S. Standard.

c) Compliance: All steel used in this work shall be certified by the Manufacturer in his proposal to be not less than Grade C as listed above.

IV-A-05 HARDWARE

All hardware, except range finders, shall be satin-finish aluminum. Clear
plastic lacquer or varnish specifically designed to protect against corrosion
due to finger prints, atmosphere, cleaning compounds, et cetera, shall be used
as a finish coat on this hardware. Range finders shall be steel, enameled
to match the end panels on which they are to be installed.

IV-A-06 WORKMANSHIP AND INSTALLATION

All parts of this bookstack installation shall be designed, fabricated and
installed, so that there will be no exposed sharp edges, corner, bolts, or
fastenings that might injure books or personnel. All adjustable shelves must
be fully inter-changeable in all units, and installation and workmanship must
be neat and proficient. All damages incurred by this Contractor, either to
the materials being installed or to the building (whether incurred in shipping
or during installation) shall be replaced or repaired to the satisfaction of
the Owner at no cost to the Owner. If, upon completion of this Contractor's
work, there still remains damages to be corrected, the Owner reserves the right

GROUP A - STEEL BOOKSTACKS
DETAILED SPECIFICATIONS

to have this work done at the expense of the Contractor. Such charges will
be deducted from the total contract amount payable to the Contractor. All
installation work described in these specifications must be under the direct
and continuous supervision of a factory-trained and experienced erection superin-
tendent who is a regular and permanent employee of the Manufacturer.

The complete installation shall be secure, level, plumb, square, true, rigid,
and accurately aligned.

Existing Remington-Rand stacks in the present Library to be removed and re-
installed on the Lower Floor of the new library as shown in the plans, Sheet No. 1. Owner will
remove books. This Contractor shall reassemble stacks, move to new Library
and install as indicated, complete with end panels. (See Alternate No. 1, Group A).

IV-A-07 TYPE OF CONSTRUCTION

The bookstacks to be furnished under this specification shall be of the type
generally shown as reinforced, bracket-type bookstack, wherein shelf-supporting
members consisting of central columns only, support the adjustable shelves in
cantilever fashion. Ranges shall be composed of sectional units so designed
that one or more compartments (sections) of any range may be removed without
affecting the stability of the remaining compartments (sections). In recoggi-
tion of the fact that different manufacturers have different d.esigns, these
specifications set forth basic criteria for performance that will enable the
manufacturer to best meet the requirements of this bookstack installation.

a) Unless otherwise noted on the drawings or in the Schedule of Equipment,
all bookstack ranges are to be full height with stack columns or uprights 90"
high. Where low shelving is called for, and not otherwise indicated, uprights
shall be approximately 42" high. All 42" high stack ranges shall be provided
with suitable one-piece, reinforced tops with high pressure plastic laminate
surfaces selected by the Owner from standard available patterns. All such
tops shall be self-edged with plastic laminate.

GROUP A - STEEL BOOKSTACKS
DETAILED SPECIFICATIONS

b)   Bookstacks on this contract in rooms 114, 201, 202, 316, 317, and 318, are
to be installed over resilient tile floors and all bookstack uprights and other
bearing surfaces shall be provided with live neoprene or natural rubber cushions
to protect the tile. All other bookstacks on this contract are to be installed
over carpeting and cushions shall be omitted. Instead the contractor shall
supply his recommended footing for carpeting.

c) All sections are to be correctly spaced by top tie channels not more than
9 feet nor less 3 feet in length, and so designed that ranges and sections can
be easily disassembled and reassembled. Tie channels shall be so punched that
the perforations in the uprights which receive shelf end brackets, run to within
1/2 inch of the extreme top of the upright.

d) All base shelves shall be not less than 3 inches nor more than 4 inches in
height, and shall be so designed that they are continuous from face to face of
the range, with no gaps between individual sections of the range. Depths of
base shelves shall be as required in the Schedule of Equipment, in which base
shelf dimensions are given in terms of nominal depths of single-faced sections.
Base shelves of all double-faced sections shall be twice the depth indicated.

e) All single-faced bookstack ranges shall be anchored to the walls with concealed angle brackets. Sway braces are not required in such ranges.

f) Each double-faced section must have a suitable device to provide for leveling
of not less than 3/4 inch in each 3-foot section. This leveling device must be
positive in action and part of the floor protection system. No shims or
similar devices will be permitted.

g) Each full-height, 90 inch high section shall have one fixed base shelf and
six adjustable shelves, unless otherwise specified in the Schedule of Equipment.
Counterheight shelving (42 inches high), shall have one fixed base shelf and
two adjustable shelves. All adjustable shelvesshall have not less than 35
inches of clear filing space between the end brackets, and shall have no more
than 2 inches between the back edges of the shelves.

GROUP A - STEEL BOOKSTACKS
DETAILED SPECIFICATIONS

IV-A-08 SHOP DRAWINGS

Shop drawings will be required to show shop and field fabrication, assembly
or erection, and general arrangement of the work. Specific items may also
require shop drawings as specified under Schedule of Equipment. Shop drawings
shall be submitted by the Contractor in triplicate and must be approved by the
Owner before work of any nature is started. If shop drawings are returned for
corrections or changes, the Contractor will resubmit as originally stated until
an approved set has been obtained, at which time production may be started.
However, the Owner's approval of shop drawings shall not be deemed binding
and the Contractor shall assume full responsibility for correctness of measurements, sizes, and materials required for all construction. Nor shall such
approval be a basis for any extra payment in case of errors or discrepancies
between shop drawings and actual job requirements. The Contractor shall be
responsible for all necessary field measurements to insure proper installation
of the bookstacks.

IV-A-09 MINIMUM MANUFACTURING AND PERFORMANCE REQUIREMENTS

While it is the intent of these specifications to obtain the very finest design, materials, and installation, it is not the intention to eliminate any
qualified bidder. The bidder is thus permitted some leeway in the use of his
procedures. Detailed requirements, essential to the proper installation of
bookstacks on this contract, are set forth below:

a) Bookstack columns for uprights may be of tubular welded construction, or
of formed and bolted construction, provided they are not less than 2 x 2 inches
in cross-section, and are fabricated of not less than 16 gauge steel. If welded,
all exposed welds shall be ground perfectly smooth. Such columns must be
perforated the full height (to within 1/2 inch of the overall height of the
stack) on both faces with slots spaced one inch on vertical centers to permit
one inch adjustment of shelves vertically. At least every sixth slot in each
row shall be different in shape from the other slots to provide a visual guide
to shelf adjustment.

GROUP A - STEEL BOOKSTACKS
DETAILED SPECIFICATIONS

b) Attachment of bookstack uprights to base brackets shall be rigidly and
neatly done with no projecting bolts or sharp corners. Each such column
support shall extend the full depth of the shelving from face to face. Leveling
devices shall be attached to base brackets to compensate for irregularities
in floor surfaces. No shims to compensate for floor irregularities will be
allowed. To provide greater rigidity and lateral stability, the base end
end brackets may extend through and be bolted to the column.

c) Base shelf and/or bottom spreaders, as well as the top tie channels shall
be designed to complement the structural system of the manufacturer, but must
align bookstack columns on 36 inch centers. Base shelves and/or spreaders
must be in three-foot units, but the top tie channels shall not exceed 9 feet
in length. Tie channels must be precision designed to perform this essential
function of alignment. No projecting nuts, bolts, or other structural fastenings or possible damaging components shall be exposed to injure book or personnel.
All necessary splices in top tie channels shall occur only at the column centers.
The closure of the base shelf to the floor may be either an integral part of the
base shelf or separate, depending upon the manufacturer's standard design. Base
shelves in double-faced sections may be of one or two piece construction. In
the latter case there shall be no cracks or slots to permit losing pamphlets
or other small items.

d) It is the intent of these specifications that the bookstacks provided on
this contract shall have maximum stability and rigidity in both lateral and
longitudinal directions. Adequate resistance to lateral stresses, such as may
be caused by eccentric loading of books, requires columns sufficiently strong
that loads up to a maximum of 1,000 pounds on one side of a full-height, double-
faced section will result in no deflection of the column in excess of 3/8 of an
inch. Similarly, the stacks shall be sufficiently rigid that a 100 pound force
applied horizontally, parallel to the range length, against the uprights at
a point 48 inches from the floor, shall result in no permanent deflection
greater than 1/16 inch from the vertical and no temporary deflection in excess
of 3/8 inch at any time during the test. (All tests conducted without end panels.)

GROUP A - STEEL BOOKSTACKS
DETAILED SPECIFICATIONS

Bidders shall certify in their proposals that the stacks to be provided on this
contract will meet the above performance standards. The Owner reserves the
right to conduct such tests on samples to be submitted by bidders and to disqualify those whose product does not meet these performance specifications.

IV-A-10 **STACK BRACING**

It is the general intent of this specification to use double-faced bookstack
ranges braced longitudinally by the use of diagonal sway braces fastened to
the uprights and adjusted by means of turnbuckles. Attachment of sway braces
to the columns must be in such a way as to eliminate any rough surfaces and must
be positive so that sway braces cannot slip out of position when tightened.
At least one pair of sway braces shall be installed in every five sections of
each range. Every range over 15 feet long shall have an additional pair of
sway braces for each five sections or fraction thereof over the 15-foot length.
This provision is not intended to disqualify the use of bookstacks specifically
designed to have the necessary stability without the use of sway braces, for
example, by the use of a welded frame, but it is intended to set up minimum
requirements for bracing.

In addition to the above bracing, double-faced ranges consisting of three
or more double-faced sections shall have transverse strut channels of not less
than 16 gauge formed steel, bolted across and at right angles to the top channels
of each double-faced range. Such transverse strut channels shall be located
36 inches from either end of the stack ranges, with a third channel centered
on the range. In areas where ranges are interrupted by rows of carrels, strut
channels shall not extend across reader space.

IV-A-11 **ADJUSTABLE SHELVES AND BRACKETS**

All adjustable steel bookstack shelves shall be formed to a 3/4 inch deep,
open box section, at both front and back edges, and have a design load of
not less than 50 pounds per square foot. Shelves for phonograph record storage
(Room 114) shall be reinforced to sustain a load of not less than 75 pounds

GROUP A - STEEL BOOKSTACKS
DETAILED SPECIFICATIONS

per square foot. Under these loads, temporary deflection shall not exceed
3/16 inch, with no permanent deflection. All brackets for bookstack shelves,
including the base shelf brackets, shall be no less than 16 gauge steel with
front and top edges formed or rolled outward not less than 1/8 inch. Since it
is the intent that there shall be minimum gaps between brackets when shelves
are hung at the same level, the actual outward roll of the bracket will depend
upon the overall shelf length. Brackets shall extend not less than 6 inches
above the top surface of the shelf. Spacers on brackets shall be used to
prevent overlapping of brackets. To make it easy to grasp the books immediately
adjacent to the shelf brackets, such brackets may be formed to a radius or cut
back at a slope to accomplish this purpose. All adjustable shelves shall be
designed so that they can be easily raised or lowered without removing the
contents from the shelf and without the necessity of completely removing the
shelf from the supporting column. To accomplish this, shelf brackets shall
be designed with no more than two hooks and no less than one hook, and they
shall have not more than two lugs nor less than one lug, in order to maintain
alignment and prevent accidental dislodgment. Shelf brackets shall be of the
hinged type, designed to fold flat to shelf for storage without being detached
from the shelf. The depth of shelves shall be as called for in the Schedule of
Equipment.

IV-A-12 SPECIAL SHELVES

a) Sliding Reference Shelves. Sliding reference shelves shall be provided
as indicated on the drawings. Such shelves shall be approximately 33 inches
long, as deep as required and shall fit under a standard shelf of a double-
faced section so that the shelf can be pulled out a minimum distance of eleven
inches.   Sliding shelf guides shall be attached to the flanges of the book
shelves without fastenings so that relocation is possible without the use of
tools. Safety stops shall be provided to prevent accidental dislodgment of
the shelf. Shelf slide assembly shall provide for smooth, quiet operation.

b) Flush Bracket (Inverted Bracket) Shelves. Flush bracket shelves shall be
supplied in those units so indicated on the drawings or called for in the
Schedule of Equipment. These shelves are to be so designed that when hung

GROUP A - STEEL BOOKSTACKS
DETAILED SPECIFICATIONS

at the same level, on the same range face, there will be no interruptions or
projections hung above the top surfaces of the shelves and materials may be
filed continuously.

c) <u>Sloping Periodical Display Shelves and Storage Shelves</u>. Sloping shelves
for the display of periodicals shall be of not less than 18 gauge steel formed
to an approximate 3/4 inch deep open box section at the top edge. The front
edge shall have an approximate 1/2 inch hem and shall be turned up to form
a U-shaped lip approximately 1-1/8 inch deep and approximately 3/4 inch high.
Sloping shelves shall be designed to hang independently on the columns and
shall have no projections above the display or sloping surface to prevent
shelving unbound periodicals flat and in continuous rows across two or more
sections of bookstack. These shelves shall be not less than 14 inches wide
from lower lip to upper edge and shall be designed to provide a display surface
not less than 60 nor more than 75 degrees from the horizontal.

Flat shelves consisting of flush-bracket shelves shall be provided for the
storage of unbound back issues of periodicals.

The design of both display and flush bracket shelves shall be such as to
provide 6 inches of clear storage space for unbound periodicals. Each section
of bookstack for periodical display shall accommodate 5 combination units of
sloping and flat shelves for periodical display and storage.

d) <u>Divider Shelves</u>. Where indicated in the <u>Schedule of Equipment</u>, certain
sections of bookstacks will be equipped with shelves having actual depths of
8 or 9 inches, with backs approximately 6 inches high. Each such shelf shall
have six adjustable dividers in addition to the end brackets. All dividers
shall be adjustable on one inch centers. All divider shelves must be inter-
changeable in all units.

GROUP A - STEEL BOOKSTACKS
DETAILED SPECIFICATIONS

Divider shelves for phonograph record storage shall be of the same general
design as those above except that both adjustable and base shelves shall be
11 inches in actual depth (i.e., shall provide full 11 inches depth for storage)
and shall have end brackets, backs, and dividers not less than 10 inches in
height. Record shelves shall be provided with twelve dividers per shelf.

e) Coat Rack Sections. Coat racks where indicated shall include standards
as specified above, top tie, and base shelf; and shall be fitted with hanger
rod and eighteen attached type coat hangers. One hat shelf above each section
shall be furnished.

IV-A-13 STEEL END PANELS

One piece finished steel end panels shall be provided for all range ends,
unless otherwise indicated on the drawings or in the Schedule of Equipment.
End panels shall be in a plain or patterned steel finish.

Such end panels shall be not less than 18 gauge steel and shall extend the
full width (face to face) of all units measured at the base shelves and shall
extend the full height of the range. End panels shall be triple-flanged at
the vertical edges. The front vertical edge of single-faced panels and both
vertical edges of double-faced panels shall be formed to not more than a
1/8 inch radius, with a return of not less than 2 inch parallel to the face
of the panel. The return shall be secured to the end bracket of the base
shelf and to a support bar at the top in a manner to eliminate any projecting
surfaces that might damage library materials. Each panel shall be reinforced
as necessary to eliminate any deflection or "oil can effect" after the panel
is secured in place. There shall be no tendency of the end panel to move
around the upright. End panels shall be continuous from one face of the range
to the other and shall have no exposed joints on the face of the end panel.

IV-A-14 PLASTIC TOPS

a) The tops of bookstacks indicated in the Schedule of Equipment 42 inches
high are to be covered with high pressure plastic laminate and self-edged.
Tops shall overhang ends 1/2 inch on front and/or back and 1 inch on ends.

GROUP A - STEEL BOOKSTACKS
DETAILED SPECIFICATIONS

Tops shall be permanently secured to metal stacks.

b) The cores of such tops shall be 1-3/16 inch thick and plastic shall be 1/16 inch thick, cemented to core on top and 4 edges. The undersides of tops shall have required extra sheet to prevent warping.

IV-A-15 ACCESSORIES

a) Range Index Holders. Range index holders shall be of 20 gauge steel formed into a V-shape and flanged on both sides of the V to receive a 5 x 3 inch card on each face. Holders shall be painted to match end panels. One such holder shall be furnished for each end panel.

b) End Label Holders. End label holders shall be made of satin finished aluminum, to hold one 5 x 3 inch card in each holder. Two such card holders shall be furnished for each double-faced end panel, and one such card holder for each single-faced end panel.

c) Book Supports. One wire-type book support shall be furnished for every standard or divider type adjustable shelf furnished on this contract except for fixed base shelves. Such wire-type book supports shall be fabricated of heavy gauge, nickel-plated, steel spring wire.

d) Clip-on Shelf Label Holders. Shelf label holders of the clip-on type to be fastened to the face of the shelf without tools shall be furnished. Holders shall be of satin-finished aluminum alloy and shall provide clear space for a label approximately 1/2 inch x 3 inches. Top of clip-on label holder shall not project above the shelf. One thousand clip-on shelf label holders are required.

IV-A-16 FINISH

All metal parts, except as specified elsewhere, shall be of the color specified below in Paragraph IV-A-17. Finish shall be a synthetic enamel applied and baked according to the manufacturer's recommendations to provide the very highest grade of enamel finish with good soil resistance, but without objectionable

GROUP A - STEEL BOOKSTACKS
DETAILED SPECIFICATIONS

sheen. All parts shall have a uniform thickness of coating inside and outside
to prevent all possibility of rusting and shall comply to the requirements
listed below.

a) Stock. All materials used shall be oiled stock completely free from
rust and all parts and exposed edges shall be dressed to a smooth surface.

b) Cleaning. All parts shall be thoroughly cleaned to remove all dirt,
grease and foreign materials. If alkaline or acid treatment has been applied,
a neutralizing rinse shall be used.

c) Pretreatment. All parts shall be phosphate treated, followed by a water
rinse, and passage through a dry-off oven.

d) Finish Coat. The finish coat shall be an alkyd-type enamel, sprayed
or dipped according to the manufacturer's recommendations to insure good even
coverage of all surfaces. Recesses not adequately reached by this method shall
be hand sprayed before baking.

e) Baking Time. Temperature cycle shall be in accordance with the manufacturer's recommendations and once established shall be maintained. Absolute
minimum film thickness for all enameled surfaces shall be 1 mil. Any deviation
shall be in excess of this minimum figure.

f) Paint Finish Performance Requirements.

    1. Testing of Paint Finish. Bookstack manufacturers shall provide a
certificate with their bids that all products to be furnished on this job will
meet the following testing procedures and that they have in fact been so tested
and have met the test requirements.

    2. Tests. Film thickness of enamel shall be measured by a General
Electric thickness gauge or equivalent (See ASTM Method D 1005-51 and ASTM
1400-58). Measurements of less than 1 mil thickness shall be considered as
failure and cause for disqualification of the sample.

GROUP A - STEEL BOOKSTACKS
DETAILED SPECIFICATIONS

a. Gloss - Gloss shall be not less than 50 nor more than 70 as determined on a 60 degree gloss meter (See ASTM Method D523-53T).

b. Bend test (adhesion) - two specimens prepared as outlined above shall be bent 180 degrees over a 1/4 inch diameter mandrel; one parallel to and one traverse to the grain of the steel, as follows: Place the coated side upper most on a mandrel at a point equi-distant from the edges of the panel and bend the panel double in approximately one second. Cracks occurring at either end and extending no more than 1/4 inch shall be disregarded.

c. Print Resistance - Panels prepared as previously described shall be subjected to the following tests:

Cold print - A piece of 2 x 2 inch cheesecloth shall be placed on the finished panel. A metal 5 pound weight shall be placed on the cloth. The contact surface of the weight shall be a smooth surface and one square inch in area. The weight shall remain unmoved in the position for 24 hours at 75 degrees F.

Hot print - The same procedure shall be used for the hot print test as used for the cold print test with the following changes;

1. The weight shall be 2 pounds instead of 5 pounds.
2. The temperature during the pressure shall be 110 degrees F. instead of 75 degrees F.

d. Impact test (adhesion and flaking) - Two specimens shall be prepared as described above. One specimen shall be placed over a 1-1/4" diameter opening. A ball of 530 gm. weight shall be dropped 10.5 inches on the section of the panel over the opening. The test shall be repeated on the other specimen on the reverse side. Cracks or hairline cracks or chipping of the impact area shall be considered a failure of the test and cause for disqualification.

e. Abrasion resistance (Taber) - Two 4 x 4 inch panels shall be prepared as described above. The film thickness shall be accurately controlled and shall be measured at four places equi-distant from the center of the panel.

GROUP A - STEEL BOOKSTACKS
DETAILED SPECIFICATIONS

The thickness shall not vary more than 0.2 mils. Weigh the panels. Place
the panel on the platform of the Taber abraser using a CS10 wheel and 2-1000
gram weights. Subject the panel to 1000 cycles cleaning the panels by brushing
every 100 cycles. Repeat with the second panel. Loss in excess of .650 grams
per 1000 cycles (average of two results) shall be considered a failure and
cause for rejection and disqualification.

       f. Salt spray - This test shall be run in accordance with ASTM
Method B287-57T, using panels prepared as previously specified. After fifty
hours of salt spray, specimens showing any evidence of discoloration, or
scratched areas showing lifting or rusting more than 1/8 inch outside of the
scribe lines shall be considered failure and cause for disqualification.

       g. Acid and chemical resistance to cleaning chemicals, etc. -
Five wells 1/2 inch in diameter and 1/2 inch deep shall be formed on the face
of test specimens with modeling clay. Into each of four individual wells, one
of the following shall be poured:

          1. Alcohol (95%)
          2. Mineral or Vegetable Oil
          3. 10% Acetic Acid
          4. Undiluted Household Ammonia

At the end of fifteen minutes, a 10% lye solution shall be poured into the
fifth well. At the end of thirty minutes from the time the first four solutions
were poured into the wells, the five wells shall be removed and the test panel
rinsed thoroughly and wiped dry. Evidence of discoloration, softening, or
blemish of the finished surface shall be considered failure and cause for
disqualification.

       h. Cigarette burns - A well-lighted cigarette shall be laid on the
finished panel and allowed to remain in one position for 1-1/2 minutes. After
removing the cigarette, the test panel shall be rinsed with water only and
wiped dry. Any evidence of stain or blemish on the finish shall be considered
failure and cause for disqualification.

GROUP A - STEEL BOOKSTACKS

DETAILED SPECIFICATIONS

IV-A-17   COLOR:

All shelves, columns, tie channels, transverse channels, and other exposed
metal parts of bookstacks on the lower floor shall be finished in _____
_____ No. 97 Gray Mist to match existing _____ bookstacks. All end
panels on this floor, including those in rooms 111, 114 and 122 shall be
_____ #65E17 Capri blue.

All other stacks throughout the Library shall have all exposed parts except
end panels in _____ No. 65E28 Champagne. End panels on these floors shall
be in accordance with the following schedule:

Room 202:	_____	65E16 Persimmon
Room 207:	_____	65E17 Capri Blue
Room 209:	_____	65E17 Capri Blue
Room 218:	_____	65E16 Persimmon
Room 219:	_____	65E16 Persimmon
Rooms 316, 317, 318:	_____	65E16 Persimmon
Room 322:	_____	65E17 Capri Blue

IV-A-18   PAINT:

Two one-quart cans of each color paint used in this bookstack installation
shall be furnished to the Owner by the manufacturer, in addition to an appropriate quantity of suitable thinner.

IV-A-19   CLEAN-UP:

Upon completion of this work all debris, excess materials, tools, etc.,
resulting from this work shall be removed from the job site and the location
of this work shall be left broom-clean. Final dusting of all shelves is the
responsibility of the general building contractor.

GROUP A - STEEL BOOKCASES
DETAILED SPECIFICATIONS

IV-A-20 <u>GUARANTEE</u>:

The manufacturer of the bookstacks furnished on this contract shall issue with
the Bid Proposal a written guarantee to the Owner stating that the bracket
type bookstacks as delivered and installed (to be installed) on this contract
were (will be) constructed and finished in accordance with these specifications.
It shall be further understood that the manufacturer will replace or repair any
and all work which may prove defective within a period of five years after
acceptance by the Owner, without expense to the Owner of any kind, ordinary
wear and tear and unusual abuse or neglect excepted.

GROUP A - STEEL BOOKSTACKS
SCHEDULE OF EQUIPMENT

Item A-1   (Room 111)
One (1) range consisting of seven (7) single-faced sections. Each section
with one (1) fixed 10-inch base shelf and six (6), 10-inch nominal (9-inch
actual) adjustable shelves of the divider type. Furnish six (6) dividers
per shelf. Furnish one (1) end panel to be installed at left end of this
range. Fasten to wall with concealed angle-brackets.

Item A-2   (Room 111)
Two (2) ranges consisting of five (5) double-faced sections each. Each d.f.
section with one (1) fixed 20-inch base shelf and twelve (12), 10-inch nominal
(9-inch actual) adjustable shelves of the divider type. Furnish six (6)
dividers per shelf. Furnish one (1) end panel for each range to be installed
at exposed end of range.

Item A-3   (Room 111)
One (1) range consisting of four (4) double-faced sections as in A-2 above.
Furnish two (2) end panels for this range.

Item A-4   (Room 114)
Two (2) ranges consisting of three (3) double-faced sections each. Each d.f.
section with one (1) fixed 24-inch base shelf and ten (10), 11-inch actual
adjustable shelves of the divider type. Each shelf shall be reinforced to
withstand a maximum load of 75 pounds per square foot with no temporary
deflection. Furnish twelve (12), 10-inch high dividers per shelf. Furnish
and install two (2) end panels each range.

DETAILED SPECIFICATIONS AND SCHEDULE OF EQUIPMENT
SECTION IV

GROUP B - TECHNICAL LIBRARY FURNITURE
DETAILED SPECIFICATIONS

IV-B-01 <u>**GENERAL**</u>:

All applicable provisions of the General Conditions govern work under this
section.

IV-B-02 <u>**SCOPE**</u>:

Perform all work necessary to complete the fabrication, shop finishing,
delivery, and installation of general furnishings and equipment as shown
on the drawings and specified herein.

The library wood furniture and technical library equipment to be furnished
under this specification is of a technical nature and designed to be manufactured for the unique requirements of the library in which it will be used.
Because of the extremely hard use to which this equipment will be subjected,
it is vital to the successful execution of the contract and to the subsequent
operation and maintenance of the library and to the future expansion of the
library, that bids be considered only from firms representing manufacturers
who specialize in the design and manufacture of library equipment and who have
made installations of comparable size and type. Each bidder shall submit
with his bid, the name and location of the factory or factories wherein the
materials covered by this section of the specifications would be manufactured,
the number of years he has been engaged in manufacturing equipment of this
character, and the name and location of recent library installations comparable
in size and type. These specifications contemplate the installation of equipment of the highest type, as measured by the standards that the library wood
furniture industry observes.

It is the intent of this contract that library furniture to be provided on
GROUP B, shall be of matching and uniform design, such design to be harmonious
with and complimentary to the design of the building. In consequence, it is
a requirement of this contract that those items listed in the <u>Schedule of</u>
<u>Equipment</u>, GROUP B, shall be designed and produced by the same manufacturer
except as noted below. Thus, no miscellaneous assortment of equipment and

GROUP B - TECHNICAL LIBRARY FURNITURE
DETAILED SPECIFICATIONS

furniture assembled by a dealer or agent from two or more manufacturers shall
be considered as meeting the requirements of these specifications, nor will
GROUP B furniture be separated and awarded in parts to two or more manufacturers
or dealers. This requirement, however, does not prevent a manufacturer from
obtaining a limited number of items from other sources, provided the quality,
finish, and leg base design (where this is pertinent) meet the requirements of
these specifications and match the equipment he produces in his own plant.
Bidders proposing to take advantage of this provision shall so indicate in their
proposals, naming items and manufacturers involved.

IV-B-03   APPROVED MANUFACTURERS:
The following manufacturers only are approved for bidding on GROUP B, Technical
Library Furniture:

a)

b)

c)

d)

e)

IV-B-04   CODE NUMBERS:
The code numbers listed in the Schedule of Equipment for GROUP B, refer to numbers shown on the floor plan, Sheet Nos. 1-3.

IV-B-05   SHOP DRAWINGS:
Shop drawings shall be submitted to Owner in triplicate for all items so indicated in the Schedule of Equipment. Shop drawings shall show finishes, designs,
dimensions, and clearly indicate in large scale, the construction of various
components, methods of assembly, thickness of materials, reinforcements, fastenings, and all other pertinent data and information. NOTE THAT THE SCHEDULE OF
EQUIPMENT REQUIRES THAT CERTAIN SHOP DRAWINGS SHALL BE SUBMITTED WITH BIDS. All
required shop drawings shall be submitted to Owner not later than four (4) weeks
after award of contract.

GROUP B - TECHNICAL LIBRARY FURNITURE

DETAILED SPECIFICATIONS

IV-B-06   UNIT PRICES:

Although GROUP B will be awarded as a group, unit prices for all items shall be shown in the bidder's proposal. Owner reserves the right to increase or decrease quantities required by an amount not to exceed ten (10%) percent.

GROUP B - TECHNICAL LIBRARY FURNITURE
DETAILED SPECIFICATIONS

IV-B-07 **MATERIALS**:

All materials used in fulfilling the requirements of this specification shall be the best of their respective kinds and those best adapted to the construction for which they are to be employed and shall meet the following general specifications:

a) **Top surfaces**. All exposed top surfaces on study tables, carrels, index tables, catalog reference tables, CBI table, bibliography shelves, map and atlas cases, and standing height dictionary stands shall be Parkwood high pressure plastic laminate 1/16 inch thick. Pattern shall be Parkwood Appalachian Cherry, No. 6060.

b) **Table tops**: Table tops may be of particle board, plywood, or lumber core construction as specified below.

Edges and corners of all table tops and other horizontal surfaces shall be square. All tables and carrels shall have flat vinyl edge strips matching in color the Appalachian Cherry plastic tops.

1) **Particle board** shall be full density and not less than 11/16 inch in thickness before application of plastic laminate exterior surface. Underside shall be covered with phenolic backing sheet thick enough to equalize panel stresses and prevent warping. Particle board table tops shall be used only in designs in which a welded frame of not less than 1-inch tubular steel supports the top on all four edges. Particle board table tops 60 x 30 inches or and larger shall be reinforced below the top by metal angles running the full length of the table and mechanically fastened to the steel frame to which the legs are welded. Such reinforcing shall not be visible when standing or sitting.

2) **Plywood**. All plywood shall be of an uneven number of plies. Where the design does not receive support from a metal frame under all four edges, such plywood shall be not less than 1-1/4 inches thick for tables up to and including 60 inches in length. Tops of all tables longer than 60 inches shall be 1-1/2 inches thick. Tops shall be properly reinforced where required with metal strips or angles.

GROUP B - TECHNICAL LIBRARY FURNITURE
DETAILED SPECIFICATIONS

Plywood for all other surfaces shall be of appropriate thickness for the purpose. Face veneers on such plywood shall be of northern grown Yellow Birch finished to match the Parkwood, Appalachian Cherry plastic surface.

3) Lumber Core. Cores for all tables and other large surfaces shall be "Lumber core plywood construction", using the best grade hardwood core stock and suitable hardwood cross bands running at right angles to the core stack. The bottom surface shall have a suitable backing sheet to equalize stresses and prevent warping of the top after application of the plastic laminate.

IV-B-08   DRYING:

All wood used in execution of this contract shall be thoroughly air-dried and kiln-dried at the fabricating point until it reaches a moisture content of approximately 5 percent, then held in dry storage until the moisture content rises to between 6 percent and 7 percent. It shall be maintained at this level during the manufacturing process. The ability of the manufacturer to control this curing and drying process throughout the entire manufacturing procedure and to maintain the proper moisture levels in the wood during fabrication is probably one of the most important phases of furniture manu- facture and the manufacturer must be equipped to handle all phases of this work under his direct supervision and must have forced-air drying kilns at the fabrication point.

IV-B-09   GLUING:

Water-resistant resin adhesives shall be used throughout and shall be cured with high frequency electronic equipment where possible and feasible. The manufacturer shall have such high frequency equipment in his factory. All such glue joints shall pass the standard test for delamination as established by the U.S. Bureau of Standards CS 35-49 (this essentially calls for complete submersion of samples to be tested at room temperature between 70° F. and 100° F. for a period of 24 hours, with the cycle being repeated, after which no noticeable failure shall be apparent.)

GROUP B - TECHNICAL LIBRARY FURNITURE
DETAILED SPECIFICATIONS

IV-B-10 <u>METAL LEGS, RAILS, AND CROSS STRETCHERS</u>:

All legs on tables, carrels, and on other furniture where designated, shall
be of 1-inch square stainless steel, 18-gauge; 1-inch square, 11-gauge cold
rolled tubular steel; or 16-gauge steel covered with an aluminum tube on the
outside. In no case shall the finished leg be less than 1-inch square or more
than 1-1/4 inches square (including aluminum tube if any). Rails and stretchers
shall be of solid aluminum or steel bars or angles of sufficient size to
provide all needed support. All legs shall be fastened to frames by welding,
and all such joints shall be ground smooth where these are visible. No
fillets will be permitted. Other fastenings of metal to metal shall be with
tamper-proof socket head cap screws. Center rails shall have rail braces
where needed to insure stability of the base frame.

IV-B-11 <u>GLIDES</u>:

All items having metal legs shall be equipped with an adjustable glide 1-1/2
inches in diameter, Bassick "No-Mar" or equal. This glide shall permit an
upward height adjustment of 1 inch from basic height.

IV-B-12 <u>CARD CATALOG CABINETS AND TRAYS</u>:

Card catalog cabinets are to be of 72-tray design and of the same construction.
All card catalog trays are to be interchangeable from one case to the an other.
Each cabinet shall have separate tops, sides, backs, and leg bases, except
see Alternate No. 2, GROUP B.

All ends, tops, backs, and bases are to be of veneered construction with
cherry, or cherry finished Yellow Birch, veneer to match the other items of
equipment in the contract. No exterior solid stock is to be exposed except
for ebonized tray fronts. Veneered surfaces are to be banded and no core
stock is to be exposed.

All trays are to be equipped with snap rods which will pass through the
lower margin of the catalog card. The front of the rod shall have a satin-
finished chrome or aluminum knob which shall engage against a bushing embedded

GROUP B - TECHNICAL LIBRARY FURNITURE
DETAILED SPECIFICATIONS

in tray front, but without any ferule. Rods shall be fitted with concealed
automatic latches allowing for removal without unscrewing or without the need
of lifting the tray when it is placed on the center of reference table.
Each tray shall be equipped with a cast, satin-finished aluminum double compart-
ment ring pull label holder. All trays shall be equipped with an adjustable
follower, so designed as to be operated easily with one hand and to be positive
in action rather than depending upon friction for holding power. Followers
shall be heavy duty and heavy gauge metal with no sharp corners.

Vertical partitions of catalog cases are to be Densi-Wood faciñg to withstand the impact of tray backs when trays are returned to the openings.

Trays shall be of birch or cherry throughout with the tray fronts to be
ebonized before finishing. All tray dovetails are to be of the hand-cut type
to ensure a maximum gluing surface. Tray bottoms are to be glued to the tray
side and no brads, nails or glue blocks shall project below the tray bottoms
as a possible source of splintering or undue wear.

IV-B-13 READING TABLES AND CARRELS:

All reading tables and carrels shall be of the sizes and styles listed in
the Schedule of Equipment. All tables shall be so constructed and designed
that clear space under the table top shall be no less than 26-1/2 inches.
Tops of tables shall be 29 inches from the floor. Design of tables shall be
such that tubular steel legs are at or near corners of tables to provide
maximum knee space for readers.

Side panels or returns on individual carrels or on the open side of tandem
carrels shall not exceed 10 inches. Refer to Sheet No. 4 for design of
tandem carrels. Individual and tandem study carrels shall have partitions
and side panels 20 inches in height. Book shelf between side panels shall
have 12 inches clear between surface of carrel and underside of shelf.

GROUP B - TECHNICAL LIBRARY FURNITURE

DETAILED SPECIFICATIONS

IV-B-14   GUARANTEE:

The Manufacturer of all library furniture and equipment furnished on this contract shall issue with his bid proposal a written guarantee that he will replace or repair any and all work which may prove defective within a period of three years after acceptance by the Owner, without expense to the Owner of any kind, ordinary wear and tear and unusual abuse or neglect excepted.

GROUP B - TECHNICAL LIBRARY FURNITURE
SCHEDULE OF EQUIPMENT

Code No.	Room No.	Quantity	Description	Unit Price	Total Price
Item B-1	111 322	3 4	Reading Table: 72" x 42" x 29" high, Parkwood Appalachian Cherry No. 6060 top; satin-finish steel frame and legs. As manufactured by: _____, No.656, or approved equal.		
Item B-2	122 219 322	24 39 40	Study Carrels: 36" x 24" x 29" high, Parkwood Appalachian Cherry No. 6060 top; satin-finish steel frame and legs. As manufactured by _____ No. 3-3-11, or approved equal.		
Item B-3	122 219 322	5 2 6	Reading Tables: 72" x 48" x 29" high, top and frame as in B-1. As manufactured by _____ No. 3-3-24, or approved equal. Submit complete shop drawings with bids.		
Item B-4	122 219 322	2 2 2	Dictionary Stand: Sloped top, 41" high at front, approximately 24" x 18". Steel frame leg base. Cherry or cherry finished Birch construction. As manufactured by _____ No. 5-2-41, or approved equal.		
Item B-5	122	1	Card Catalog Cabinet: 30-tray unit with steel frame leg base. Yellow Birch, cherry finished or American Cherry. As manufactured by _____ No. 5-2-11, or approved equal.		
Item B-6	122	1	Record Browsing Tub: Approximately 39" x 16" x 39" high at the top. Steel frame leg base. Finished to match other furniture. See Sheet No. 4 for general design. Shop drawings required before manufacture.		
Item B-7	202	1	Cumulative Book Index table: approximately 90" x 40" x 29" high. Unit to have facilities for storing 9 volumes of CBI in open position on pull-out shelves and fixed top shelf for storing small volumes in upright position. Steel frame leg base. Finish to match other units. Submit shop drawings to Owner before manufacture.		

DETAILED SPECIFICATIONS AND SCHEDULE OF EQUIPMENT
SECTION IV

GROUP C - STEEL OFFICE FURNITURE
DETAILED SPECIFICATIONS

IV-C-01   GENERAL CONDITIONS:
All applicable portions of the GENERAL CONDITIONS apply to items furnished
on GROUP C.

IV-C-02   SCOPE:
Perform all work necessary to complete the fabrication, shop finishing,
delivery and installation of steel office furnishings and equipment as
shown on the drawings and specified herein.

IV-C-03   APPROVED MANUFACTURERS:
The following manufacturers only are approved for bidding on GROUP C,
Steel Office Furniture:

a)

b)

c)

d)

e)

IV-C-04   INFORMATION TO BE FURNISHED WITH BIDS:
The Bidder shall submit a unit price for each item of furniture included
in the Base Bid.

IV-C-05   CODE NUMBERS:
Code numbers listed in the GROUP C, Schedule of Equipment, refer to
numbers shown on the drawings for identification of each item of furniture.

IV-C-06   SHOP DRAWINGS:
Provide shop drawings as required in Schedule of Equipment.

GROUP C - STEEL OFFICE FURNITURE

DETAILED SPECIFICATIONS

IV-C-07   METAL DESKS:

A. General: Desks covered by this specification are to be designed and constructed with standardized interchangeable parts that may be rearranged and
substituted at any time, as changing layouts and conditions may require, as
follows:

    1. A vertical file drawer may be substituted for any 2 full-height box
drawers in either pedestal or vice versa.

    2. Desk understructure to be flush with face of top. Overhang can be
provided at ends or rear, when required.

    3. File and box drawers are to be interchangeable for position in pedestal.

    4. The desk pedestal shall be so constructed that a file drawer mounted
on full progressive suspension may be easily installed at any time in the field.

B. Finishes and Tops: All desks shall have high pressure plastic laminate
top selected from manufacturer's standard patterns. All desks shall have
stainless steel binding edge. Finishes shall be in mar-resistant baked acrylic
enamel; color selected from manufacturer's custom or standard finishes. Leg
uprights and hardware shall be in brushed chrome or aluminum.

C. Accessories: All desks shall be equipped with the following: one movable
partition in each box drawer, purse hook in kneespace, adjustable glides on
legs. Convenience tray in one box drawer, progressive suspension file drawer
with compressor, one sliding reference shelf with Plexiglas cover, and lock
on file drawer only.

IV-C-08   METAL FILES:

A. General: Four-drawer standard files shall be not less than 52-3/8" high
and 28-1/2" deep, with available clear filing space of 27-3/8" per drawer.

GROUP C - STEEL OFFICE FURNITURE
DETAILED SPECIFICATIONS

B. Hanging Folder Frames: All file drawers shall be designed and constructed to receive hanging folder-type frames or sway blocks where required,
without any mechanical or structural changes.

Hanging folder frames for use in filing cabinet drawers shall be constructed
of 1/8" x 5/8" band iron, zinc plated. The frames shall consist of 2 lateral
strips to carry the folder hanger which shall be so formed at the front to
fit the notches formed in the drawer head and shall have 2 upright strips
at the rear, bolted to drawer back.

C. Sway Block Construction: Sway blocks shall be made of one piece of not
less than 20 gauge steel with the top edge beaded and a formed wire section
enclosed in a rubber or plastic tube inserted into the bead. The rubber or
plastic shall make contact with the top edge of the drawer body and limit
the tilt of the sway block. The sway blocks shall have stiffening ribs
embossed in them for additional strength.

At the bottom of each sway block, in the center, there shall be electro-welded
in place, a projecting lug of not less than 18 gauge steel that shall inter-
member with the sway block retaining channel as described below.

D. Sway Block Retaining Channel: The retaining channel shall be of not less
than 20 gauge steel and be provided to be placed in the groove in the drawer
bottom. Channel shall have the top edges flanged inwardly and provided with
slots on not less than 1" centers, which shall receive the projecting lugs
on bottom of the sway block. Sway blocks shall have a tilt of approximately
20° forward and backward and shall be so designed that they will be held
securely in place and yet may be easily removed by lifting one side.

E. Suspension: Drawer suspensions shall be of the full progressive, ball-
bearing type. Case channels, suspension channels and drawer runner channels
shall be not less than 16 gauge steel. All steel used in case channels,
drawer channels and suspension channels shall be a special 1/2 hard, tempered,
cold-rolled, strip steel especially rolled for this purpose, accurately formed
or cold drawn to exact size. Suspension and drawer channels shall be nickel
or zinc plated.

GROUP C - STEEL OFFICE FURNITURE
DETAILED SPECIFICATIONS

Suspensions shall be of the "cradle type" with each pair of suspension channels connected together by 2 steel cross-angles, one 14 gauge at the center and one 16 gauge at the rear; electro-welded in place. Cross-members at the front will not be acceptable.

Each suspension shall operate on not less than two 5/8", four 9/16" and two 1/2" diameter case hardened and polished steel balls and two 5/8" diameter "floating" rollers. The two 1/16" diameter balls at the rear of the suspension shall prevent any "tip-up" of the front of a drawer that is heavily loaded at the rear.

Suspensions shall be so designed that the "floating" balls and rollers shall be self-aligning. The suspension shall be so constructed that the drawers shall close without rebound, without requiring the use of a latching device. Drawers shall stop silently and smoothly against resilient bumpers when opened and closed. Metal-to-metal stops will not be acceptable.

Drawers shall be easily removed and replaced from suspensions by lifting front of drawer. Suspensions shall be easily removed from case by lifting front of suspension. All drawers with a 65 pound load shall open with not more than 36 ounce pull.

F. <u>Hardware</u>: All hardware shall be in brushed aluminum or brushed chrome finish.

G. <u>Finishes</u>: Finishes shall be in mar-resistant, baked acrylic enamel, color to be selected from manufacturer's custom or standard finishes.

IV-C-09   <u>CHAIRS</u>:

A. <u>Fabric</u>: All fabrics shall be 100% Nylon, weave and color to be selected from manufacturer's standard fabrics, or of the best grade expanded vinyl in color as selected by Owner.

B. <u>Casters</u>: Wherever casters are required, they shall be 2-1/2 inches in diameter with hard composition wheels.

GROUP C — STEEL OFFICE FURNITURE
DETAILED SPECIFICATIONS

C. Finishes: All exposed metal shall be in brushed aluminum or brushed
chrome. Brushed aluminum finishes shall be/clear epoxy coated for protection.

D. Bases: All chair bases shall be in brushed aluminum or brushed chrome.
Brushed aluminum bases shall be/clear epoxy coated for protection.

E. Glides: All side chairs shall be furnished with stainless steel rubber
cushioned glides not less than 15/16 inch in diameter.

GROUP C - STEEL OFFICE FURNITURE

SCHEDULE OF EQUIPMENT

Code No.	Room	Quantity	Description	Unit Price	Total Price
Item C-1	102	1	Double Pedestal Desk: with 1 box drawer and 1 file drawer with lock on the left and 3 box drawers on the right; 30-1/2" x 16-1/4" typewriter unit on right side; as manufactured by _____ No. 2221 + 41-ATT-22, or approved equal by _____ _____ or _____.		
	104	1			
	105	1			
	202	2			
Item C-2	103	1	Double Pedestal Desk: as shown above, but with 1 box drawer and 1 file drawer with lock on the right and 3 box drawers on the left; typewriter unit on left side; as manufactured by _____ No. 2221 + 41-ATT-22, or approved equal by _____ or _____.		
	202	4			
Item C-3	102	1	Swivel Chair: upholstered arms, with coil spring seats, foam rubber padding seat and back rests, as manufactured by _____ No. 410-311, or approved equal by _____ _____ or _____.		
	103	1			
	104	1			
	114	1			
	207	1			
	302-308	7 (1 each rm)			
	319	1			
Item C-4	102	1	Side Chair: with upholstered arms, coil spring seats, foam rubber padding on seats and back rests, as manufactured by_____ No. 410-416, or approved equal by _____ _____ or _____.		
	103	1			
	104	1			
	302-308	7 (1 each rm)			
	319	1			
Item C-5	102	1	Lateral File: 42" wide, legal size, 5 openings (4 drawers, top opening with shelf), equipped with lock. Top shelves and drawers equipped with sway blocks. Drawers equipped with built-in framework for hanging file folders, as manufactured by_____ No. 860-561 or approved equal by _____ _____ or _____.		
	103	1			
	104	1			
	105	2			
	202	2			
	210	1			

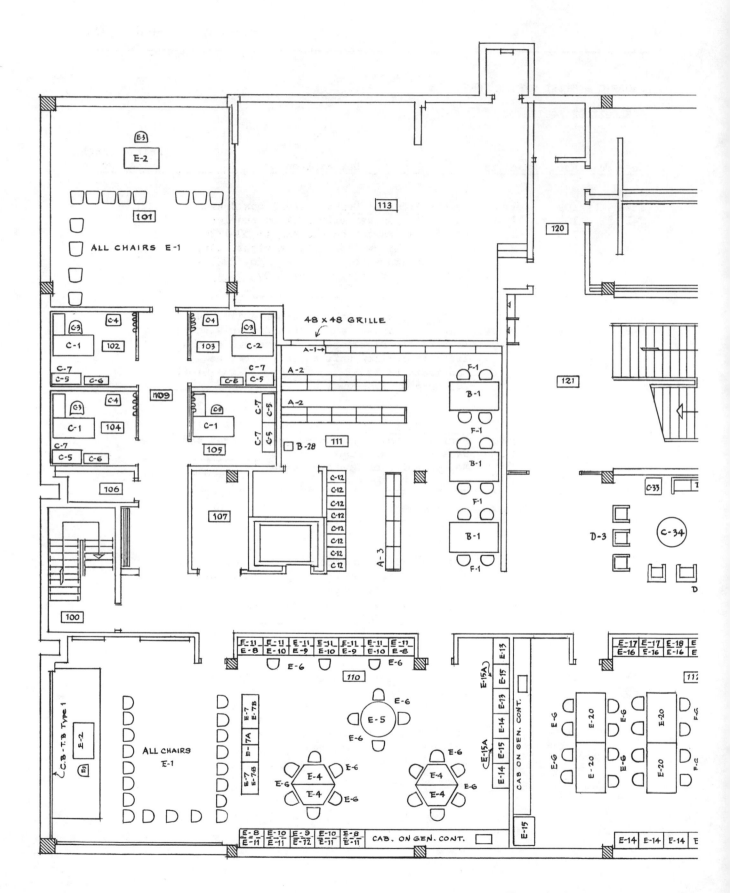

Figure 1. An example of a floor plan

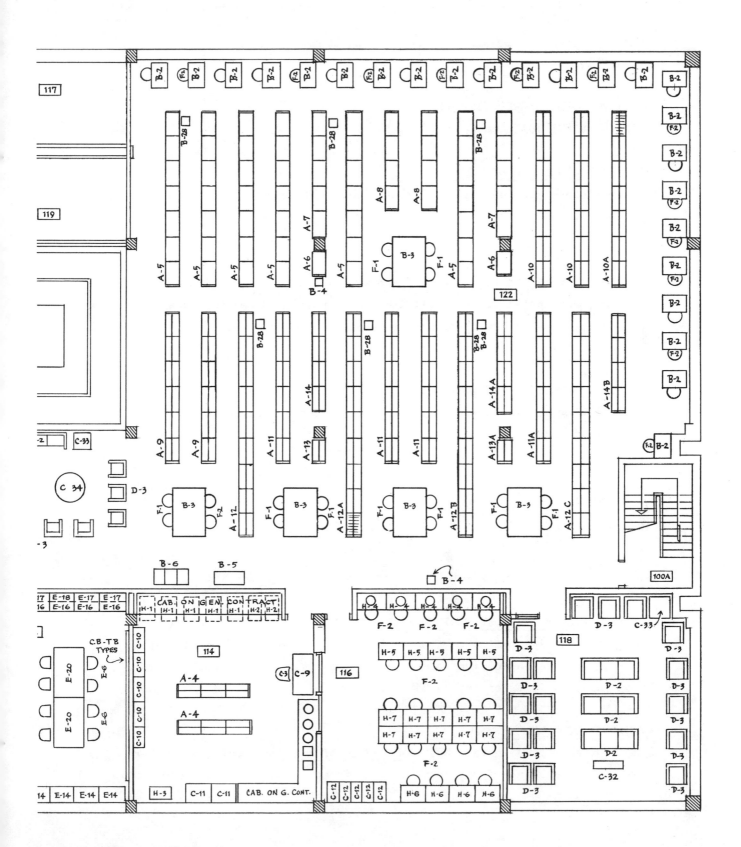

coded to furnishings specifications

DETAILED SPECIFICATIONS AND SCHEDULE OF EQUIPMENT
SECTION IV

GROUP D - UPHOLSTERED SEATING
DETAILED SPECIFICATIONS

IV-D-01   GENERAL CONDITIONS:

All applicable portions of the GENERAL CONDITIONS apply to items furnished
on GROUP D.

IV-D-02   SCOPE:

Perform all work necessary to complete the fabrication, shop finishing,
delivery, and installation of all items of upholstered seating shown on
the drawings, Sheet Nos. 1-3, and as specified herein.

IV-D-03   APPROVED MANUFACTURERS:

The following manufacturers only are approved for bidding on GROUP D,
Upholstered Seating:

a)

b)

c)

d)

e)

IV-D-04   INFORMATION TO BE FURNISHED WITH BIDS:

The Bidder shall submit a unit price for each item of upholstered seating
required in these specifications. However, award of the contract will
be on the total bid for this GROUP only.

IV-D-05   CODE NUMBERS:

Code numbers listed in the GROUP D Schedule of Equipment refer to numbers
shown on the drawings for identification of each item of upholstered seating.

GROUP D - UPHOLSTERED SEATING
DETAILED SPECIFICATIONS

IV-D-06   <u>CONSTRUCTION</u>:

Equipment furnished on GROUP D shall have welded frames of 1 inch square
tubular steel, chair legs shall be placed directly under arms to increase
stability of seating, styling shall be straight line and contemporary,
but shall not be massive or heavy.

Seat, back, and arm frames shall be of select hardwood with best
glue and dowel construction. Cross members shall be contoured so that
seats will not "bottom." Webbing shall be Pirelli in "latticework"
pattern close enough to provide maximum strength, durability, and resil-
ience. Seat padding shall be no less than 3 inches thick and of finest
pincore latex foam rubber. Back padding shall be of the same material,
no less than 2 inches thick.

IV-D-07   <u>UPHOLSTERY</u>:

Fabrics shall be 100% nylon, to be chosen from manufacturer's standard
colors, Scotchgard treated for soil resistance. Vinyls shall be best
grade expanded vinyl. Tufting, where specified, shall use nylon cord
and shall be blocked to prevent buttons from working loose or pulling
out. Welt lines shall be square and true. All tailoring shall be carefully and accurately done.

GROUP D - UPHOLSTERED SEATING
SCHEDULE OF EQUIPMENT

Code No.	Room No.	Quantity	Description	Unit Price	Total Price
Item					
D-1	301	2	Settee: Two-seater with fully up-		
	322	1	holstered arms, fixed cushions, width between arms 48", seat height 16-1/2", seat depth 20-1/2", brushed chrome finish on legs and frame, as manufactured by _____ No. 2282, or approved equal by _____. or _____		
Item					
D-2	118	3	Settee: Three-seater with fully up-		
	122	1	holstered arms, fixed cushions, width		
	203	1#	between arms 72", seat height 16-1/2",		
	208	1*	seat depth 20-1/2", brushed chrome		
	213	4*	finish on legs and frame, as manu-		
	218	1	factured by _____ No. 2286, or		
	219	1	approved equal by_____ or _____.		
Item					
D-3	118	17	Club Chair: Fully upholstered arms,		
	122	10	fixed cushions, width between arms		
	218	6	24", seat height 16-1/2", seat depth		
	219	8	20-1/2", brushed chrome finish on		
	301	8	legs and frame, as manufactured by _____		
	320	4	No. 2278, or approved equal by _____		
	322	16	or _____.		

Tufted expanded vinyl
* Tufted 100% nylon fabric

DETAILED SPECIFICATIONS AND SCHEDULE OF EQUIPMENT
SECTION IV

GROUP E - READING CHAIRS
DETAILED SPECIFICATIONS

IV-E-01   GENERAL CONDITIONS:
All applicable portions of the GENERAL CONDITIONS apply to items furnished
on GROUP E.

IV-E-02   SCOPE:
Perform all work necessary to complete the fabrication, shop finishing,
delivery, and installation of all reading chairs shown on the drawings
and as specified and listed herein.

IV-E-03   APPROVED MANUFACTURERS AND DESIGNS:
Because the design and construction of chairs suitable for library use
at tables and carrels is critical to the successful furnishing of the
new library, the owner has pre-selected those chair designs which are
acceptable on this contract. No request for approval of an alternate
chair design will be accepted unless made in writing as required under
II-12, and accompanied by a sample of the chair for which approval is
requested.

     Chair designs and manufacturers approved for bidding on this contract are
as follows:

Manufacturer	Design No.	Finish
a)		
b)		
c)		
d)		

IV-E-04   INFORMATION DESIRED FROM BIDDERS:
Bidders shall submit unit prices for chairs they propose to furnish on
this contract upholstered in _____100% nylon fabric. (Samples of manufacturer's available colors shall be submitted with proposals.)

GROUP E - READING CHAIRS
SCHEDULE OF EQUIPMENT

Code No.	Room	Description	Unit Price	Quantity	Total Price
E-1		Armless reading chair in accordance with specifications above:		96	
E-2		Arm chair in accordance with specifications above:		193	

DETAILED SPECIFICATIONS AND SCHEDULES OF EQUIPMENT

SECTION IV

GROUP F - DRAPERIES
DETAILED SPECIFICATIONS

IV-F-01   GENERAL CONDITIONS:

All applicable portions of the General Conditions apply to items furnished on Group F.

IV-F-02   SCOPE:

Provide all labor, materials, equipment, and incidentals necessary for fabricating and installing draperies where indicated and specified herein. All workmanship shall be first-class and in the best manner known to the trade.

IV-F-03   MEASUREMENTS:

All draperies are described by window and ceiling dimensions and are identified by room numbers and location of windows. Measurements given are approximate and shall be verified by the contractor before ordering any material or fabricating any work.

IV-F-04   SAMPLES:

The contractor shall submit a sample of normal fabric width and at least one yard in length, representing the material and workmanship of a typical fabric panel, including pleats, hems, and seams, proposed for this work. This sample will be used as a standard for the work to be executed and must meet the Owner's approval prior to beginning fabrication of the draperies.

IV-F-05   ADJUSTMENTS:

Final adjustments to all draperies shall be made not earlier than 30 days nor later than 60 days after installation.

IV-F-06   MATERIALS AND TRACK:

The fabric for all draperies in Rooms 208, 209, 213, 218, 219, and 313 shall be "Lattice" No. K106 (Oatmeal), 100% linen casement, Leno construction, as manufactured by _____, or approved equal.

GROUP F - DRAPERIES

DETAILED SPECIFICATIONS

Draperies shall be unlined, flameproofed, mildewproofed, and guaranteed dimensionally stable.

For all fabrics to be used in Rooms 102, 103, 104, and 105, allow $5.00 per yard. Owner will select pattern from fabrics available to the contractor, including those available from _____.

          Material allowance shall include treatment for flameproofing and mildewproofing. At time of installation, contractor shall furnish owner with certificate showing that above treatment has been completed.

Track for Rooms 102, 103, 104, and 105 shall be _____ No. 9050, extruded, etched, and anodized aluminum, in natural finish, complete with all necessary traverse equipment including master carriers, two, ball-bearing carriers per foot of track, cord tension pulley, and pulley sets. Drapery and track shall be designed for one-way draw. Bracket projection shall be 3 inches.

Track for Rooms 208, 209, 213, 218, and 219 is supplied on building contract. Drapery contractor shall supply track in Room 313.(_____ no. 9050 or equal.)

IV-F-07   MAKE-UP:
a) All draperies shall be unlined.
b) All draperies shall be Tabled.
c) All selvages shall be trimmed off.
d) French seams shall be used to sew panels together. Fold over about 3/8" so that all raw edges are in the seam.
e) Bottom hems shall be 4" double hems. No open pockets front or back.
f) Side hems shall be 1½" and shall be double.
g) B uckram shall be 4" Conso Permanent Crinoline, _____ no. 1104, or Crindurex by _____.
h) The fabric shall be folded double around the crinoline at the headings.
i) Pleats shall be French pleats. Spacing shall be not more than 4-1/2" maximum and not less than 3-3/4" apart.
j) Pleats shall be spaced evenly. Pleats shall be pinched 3 to 4 times, depending upon the weight of the fabric. Fullness shall be 100%. Pleats shall be pinched at the top and tacked in place by three double thread stitches through both fabric and crinoline.

GROUP F – DRAPERIES

DETAILED SPECIFICATIONS

k) Weights shall be 1" square lead. To be covered with sateen case and shall
be sewn in 1/2" above bottom of hem. Attach with 4 threads at top and
4 threads at bottom of weight.

l) Only best quality thread shall be used. Colors shall match colors of
the fabric.

m) Hooks shall be #1036, manufactured by _____.

n) Unlined draperies shall be machine stitched, with the exception of the
bottom hems.

o) All draperies and curtains shall be made so that they hang straight
and true.

GROUP F - DRAPERIES
DRAPERY SCHEDULE

Room Nos. 102, 103, 104, and 105:

One inside window each room each measuring 6'-0" from door casement to
corner, 7'-4" from floor to top of window frame. One-way draw in these
rooms. Top of drapery shall be 2" above top of window. Draw cord on left
in Rooms 102 and 104, on the right in Rooms 103 and 105.

Room No. 208:

One west window, measuring 15'-6" side to side, 9'-0" top of window,
9'-4" floor to ceiling. Top of drapery shall hang 1/2" below ceiling line.

Room No. 209:

One south window measuring 21'-0" side to side, 9'-0" floor to top of
window, 9'-4" floor to ceiling. Top of drapery shall hang 1/2" below
ceiling line.

Room No. 213:

Three south windows, each measuring 21'-0" side to side, 9'-0" floor to
top of window, 9'-4" floor to ceiling. Top of draperies shall hang 1/2"
below ceiling line.

Room No. 218:

One east window measuring 15'-6" side to side, 9'-0" floor to top of
window, 9'-4" floor to ceiling. Top of draperies shall hang 1/2" below
ceiling line.

Room No. 219:

One north window measuring 21'-0" side to side, 9'-0" floor to top of
window, 9'-4" floor to ceiling. Top of draperies shall hang 1/2" below
ceiling line.